HIPPOCR

Civil War Sites

Other Books by Tom Weil

A Clearing in the Jungle (1979)

A Balance of Power (1981)

Last at the Fair: A Book of Travel (1986)

America's Heartland: A Travel Guide to the Back Roads of Illinois, Indiana, Iowa and Missouri (1989)

America's South: A Travel Guide to the Eleven Southern States (1990)

The Cemetery Book: Graveyards, Catacombs and Other Travel Haunts Around the World (1992)

The Mississippi River: Nature, Culture and Travel Sites Along the "Mighty Mississip" (1992)

America's Heartland: A Travel Guide to the Back Roads of Illinois, Indiana, Iowa, Missouri and Kansas (2d edition, 1992)

America's South: The Atlantic States (2d edition, 1993)

America's South: The Gulf and the Mississippi States (2d edition, 1994)

HIPPOCRENE
U.S.A.

GUICE

to

CIVIL WAR SITES

Tom Weil

HIPPOCRENE BOOKS

New York

This book is for my London friends,
Henry and Kathrine Jackson,
with great affection

Photos courtesy of Virginia Department of Conservation and Economic
Development, National Park Service, South Carolina Division of Tourism, North Carolina Travel and Tourism Division, Kentucky Department
of Travel Development, and Pea Ridge National Military Park.

The two chapters "Civil War Sites in the Atlantic States" and "Civil War
Sites in the Gulf and the Mississippi States" previously appeared in *America's South: The Atlantic States* (1993) and *America's South: The Gulf and
the Mississippi States* (1994), both published by Hippocrene Books.

For information, address:
Hippocrene Books, Inc.
171 Madison Ave.
New York, NY 10016

Library of Congress Cataloging-in-Publication Data
Weil, Tom.
    Hippocrene U.S.A. guide to Civil War sites / Tom Weil.
        p.   cm.
    Includes index.
    ISBN 0-7818-0302-0 (paper) : $14.95
    1. United States—Civil War 1861-1865—Battlefields—
Guidebooks.   I. Title.   II. Title: Hippocrene USA guide to Civil War
sites.
E641.W47   1994
973.7—dc20   94-31935
                                                                                  CIP
Printed in the United States of America.

Contents

About This Book

Walt Whitman called the conflict "a strange sad war," and Southerners labeled it the War Between the States and "The Lost Cause," while others named it the War of the Rebellion and War for Southern Independence. By whatever name, the Civil War was no doubt the nation's most traumatic, tragic and fascinating episode.

More Americans lost their lives—620,000 dead, plus nearly 1.1 million casualties—than during the two World Wars combined. Hundreds of battlefields, historic buildings, displays, monuments, markers, memorials, cemeteries, geographic features and other remnants from the years 1861 to 1865 recall the bloody conflict.

This book focuses on Civil War sites in the region where the fighting took place. The heart of the book covers the eleven Southern states plus the border states of Missouri, Kentucky and Maryland. Kentucky appears in the section devoted to the Gulf and the Mississippi states, while Missouri and Maryland form part of the section entitled "Civil War Sites in Northern Areas." That section also lists the most significant sites in the Union areas located just to the north of the states where the main action occurred. This includes sites in Illinois, Indiana, West Virginia, Pennsylvania and the District of Columbia. The book thus gives a detailed listing of sites in all the states of the Confederacy and the border states, as well as places in nearby states and Washington, D.C., all of which comprise what might be called the main "catchment" area of the War.

In a number of places where the scene of action is described without reference to a specific site, the visitor will find an historic plaque or notice—not specifically mentioned in the text—recounting the event. While most of the sites listed offer places which the traveler can visit, some only recall where an interesting, important or unusual War event occurred but where nothing remains to evidence the episode. Although all major sites and battlefields are listed, descriptions of the most famous places—about which much has already been written—have been kept brief in order to leave room to include a number of more obscure places perhaps less familiar to many readers and travelers. Sites under each locale are for the most part listed in the order of their significance.

A guidebook whose material is arranged by location and alphabetically lacks chronological cohesion. War events in the lists which comprise this book appear where—rather than when—they happened. In order to help readers place episodes in their temporal context, the book includes a brief overview of the conflict with an account of how the War developed year by year. This general description of the War's progression will hopefully serve to provide a sense of how some of the places and events in the lists fit into the overall scheme.

The Civil War has exerted on the psyche of the nation an endless fascination. An estimated 65,000 books, along with innumerable articles, deal with the War. This book contains a list of more than 1300 sites at nearly 650 different locations recalling the epic conflict which so tormented the land—a War whose memories still haunt countless corners of the country 130 years later.

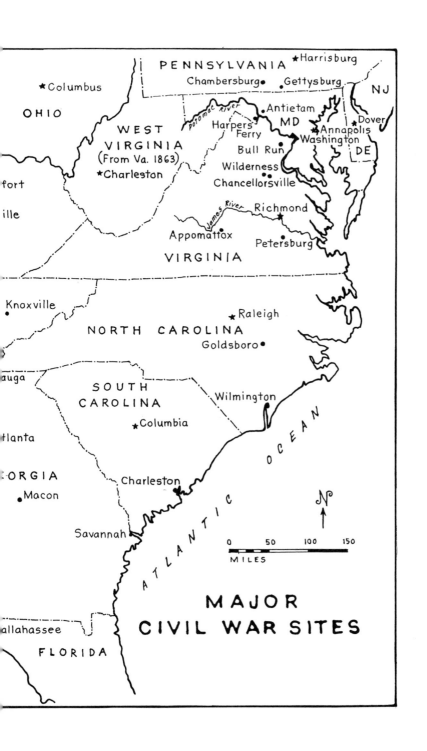

PENNSYLVANIA ★Harrisburg

★Columbus

OHIO

Chambersburg• •Gettysburg

NJ

WEST VIRGINIA (From Va. 1863)
★Charleston

Potomac River

Harpers Ferry

•Antietam

MD

Annapolis
Washington

Dover

DE

Bull Run

Wilderness
Chancellorsville

fort

ille

James River

Richmond

Appomattox•

Petersburg•

VIRGINIA

Knoxville
•

★Raleigh

NORTH CAROLINA

Goldsboro•

auga

SOUTH CAROLINA

Wilmington

★Columbia

ATLANTIC OCEAN

tlanta

ORGIA

Charleston

•Macon

Savannah

N

0   50   100   150

MILES

MAJOR
CIVIL WAR SITES

allahassee

FLORIDA

Chapter I

An Overview of the Civil War

In his March 4, 1861, inaugural address, Abraham Lincoln asserted that "the union of these states is perpetual....No state upon its mere motion can lawfully get out of the Union." Earlier, Robert Toombs of Georgia, in his valedictory address to the U.S. Senate before departing for his new nation, the Confederacy, said, "Keep us in the Union by force? Come and do it!" The North took up the challenge when Lincoln tried to provision Fort Sumter in Charleston, South Carolina. At 4:30 a.m. the morning of April 12 a ten-inch mortar at a Confederate shore battery fired the War's first shot. "The shell soared in a high arc, its burning fuse spitting like a small rocket," wrote W.A. Swanberg in *First Blood: The Story of Fort Sumter*. "It curved downward and burst almost directly over Fort Sumter. A few watchers on Charleston's Battery later swore that when it exploded it formed a pattern in flame of an almost perfect palmetto." So began the great conflict, with disastrous consequences neither side could then imagine. "The most important single explanation for the coming of the Civil War is undoubtedly the simplest one: so few, North or South, had the haziest conception of what sort of war it would be," wrote Bruce and William Catton in *Two Roads to Sumter*.

At the beginning of the War, the North and the South assessed their positions. The Union, summarized Colonel G.F.R. Henderson in *The Civil War: A Soldier's View*, viewed the following geographical and political aspects as the most important elements in devising a strategic plan: (1) the South's long coast line and small number of harbors; (2) the Mississippi River; (3) the northwest corner of Virginia, a pro-Union area (by 1863, West Virginia), which ran up into the heart of the North; (4) the proximity of the two capitals, less than 100 miles apart; (5) the Shenandoah Valley, which supplied Virginia with food and afforded a protected approach into Maryland to a point near Washington; (6) the border states of Maryland, Missouri and Kentucky ("I hope I have God on my side, but I must have Kentucky," Lincoln said).

As for the South, Archer Jones in *Civil War Command and Strategy* notes: "For the Confederates the goal was simply to keep what they had. By establishing its independence, the South had started the war victorious and need only hold onto what secession had given it and, if possible, add Missouri and Kentucky." Based on these assessments, the overriding strategies of each combatant fell into place. The Union needed to blockade Southern ports; to exert control over key areas in Virginia, such as the state's northwest corner and the Shenandoah Valley, and eventually to capture Richmond; and to gain control of the Mississippi River Valley and the border states. The Confederacy, meanwhile, needed simply to retain the territory it had carved out of the Union, now a disunion.

The War in the East in 1861 began to unfold in western Virginia when Union general George B. McClellan led his troops to victories at Philippi (June 3), Rich Mountain (July 11) and Carrick's Ford (July 13). The main focus, however, involved the Confederate capital. Goaded by Horace Greeley's *New York Tribune*, which regularly ran a headline urging "Forward to Richmond," Lincoln came under pressure for action. The North's first (of many) attempts to capture Richmond began in mid-July 1861 when General Irvin McDowell crossed the Potomac and headed south with 35,000 men. Advancing to a strategic rail junction at Manassas, a village near Bull Run Creek, McDowell on July 21 attacked the Confederates. The Rebels successfully drove the Northerners back with the help of a brigade led by Thomas J. Jackson, who withstood the assault like a "stone wall." This Union defeat in the conflict's first major battle "had incalculable repurcussions throughout the remainder of the war," stated Paddy Griffith in *Battle Tactics of the Civil War*. "Its importance cannot be overstated...because it set the tone for everything that was to follow. Having lost the first major contest the Federals formed a low opinion of themselves and a correspondingly high opinion of the Confederates."

Thus it was that when Lincoln appointed McClellan to replace McDowell, the new army commander—greatly fearing the prowess and size of the Confederate forces—spent the rest of the year recruiting and training an army of 130,000 soldiers, the largest fighting force ever assembled in the Western Hemisphere. Meanwhile, the Union navy—"Uncle Sam's web feet," Lincoln called it—managed to capture Port Royal, South Carolina, on November 7 and to begin the blockade along the Atlantic coast. But the army remained inert. McClellan kept recruiting and drilling, but not fighting. "His Army of the Potomac was a dazzling drill-ground performer, but McClellan apparently had no desire to soil their uniforms in the mud of Virginia," noted Nancy and Dwight Anderson in *The Generals: Ulysses S. Grant and Robert E. Lee*. McClellan's other fault was his fixation on the East and failure to recognize the significance of the other major theater of the War, the area beyond the Appalachians. As Joseph P. Cullen observed in *The Peninsula Campaign*, "McClellan never did appreciate the importance of the strategy in the west—in one of his letters he stated the western action would be a 'mere bagatelle'—obsessed as he was with the idea of conquering Richmond. The fact that the war would ultimately be won and lost in the west was something he failed completely to comprehend."

Out in the West in 1861 War activities soon reached the two crucial border states, Missouri and Kentucky. Irredeemably split, Missouri mirrored the larger breach which had divided the Union. Southern sympathizers vied for control of Missouri with anti-slavery advocates, greatly influenced by the state's large German population, so vehement in their views that "they seemed to outabolitionize even the New Englanders," wrote Arthur Charles

Cole in *The Irresponsible Conflict.* Missouri, "by far the richest and strongest trans-Mississipi state" was "of cardinal importance to the salvation of the Union," wrote Allan Nevins in *The War for the Union.* "Thus Missouri found herself in the peculiar position of being in two nations at once," for both North and South claimed the state, whose allegiance would soon be decided by force of arms. Union officer Nathaniel Lyon took control of the Federal arsenal in St. Louis as Governor Claiborne Fox Jackson declared Missouri part of the Confederacy. On June 15 Lyon captured Jefferson City, the state capital, and on August 10 he died—the first Union general killed in the War—at the Battle of Wilson's Creek in southwestern Missouri, the first major encounter in the West. Fighting continued at Lexington, as the balance gradually shifted to the Union side. The North, however, suffered a minor defeat on November 7 when a Union force of 3000 men (advancing from a major Federal base in Cairo, Illinois) attacked a Confederate force at Belmont, Missouri, on the Mississippi River. The leader of the Union expedition was a little known officer named Ulysses S. Grant, who at Belmont participated in his first battle of the War.

Although a minor encounter, Belmont proved to be a "crucial diversion," as Nathaniel C. Hughes noted in *The Battle of Belmont,* for the threat of a thrust by the North down the river alarmed General Leonidas Polk at the Confederate fortress just across the Mississippi on the bluffs at Columbus, Kentucky. Polk "dug in deeper and deeper," encouraging Grant to attack elsewhere. In February 1862 he captured Forts Henry and Donelson in Tennessee just below the Kentucky border.

Although the Kentucky legislature had voted for the state to remain neutral, on September 3 Confederate forces occupied Columbus, provoking Grant to enter Paducah three days later. At Columbus the Rebels established a well armed position overlooking the Mississippi. Along the river to the south the Confederates installed other similarly fortified outposts to control the Mississippi at Fort Pillow in Tennessee, Vicksburg in Mississippi, and Port Hudson in Louisiana. Noted John D. Milligan in *Gunboats Down*

the Mississippi, "This meant that the Confederates were depending
on a strategy of fixed positions to defeat one of movement,"
movement masterminded, for the most part, by Grant, who eventually gained control of the Mississippi for the North.

As 1862 opened in the East, McClellan continued to train his
troops as Lincoln grew ever more impatient for action. McClellan
"meant to advance with an army so overwhelming that he would
be irresistible," wrote T. Harry Williams in *McClellan, Sherman
and Grant.* The delay originated because McClellan persisted in
fearing that his forces would be resistible. Along the Atlantic coast
Union forces—continuing their attempt to capture ports and
mount a blockade—took Roanoke Island on February 8 and New
Bern, North Carolina, on March 14. Three days later McClellan
finally began the Peninsular Campaign, transferring by ship the
Army of the Potomac to the peninsula in Virginia formed by the
James and the York Rivers. The army would then advance up the
peninsula to Richmond.

On March 9, just before the army was transferred to the peninsula, battle was joined in the area when the *Merrimack* and the
Monitor ironclads clashed in Hampton Roads off the tip of the
peninsula. The *Monitor's* neutralization of the South's warship gave
McClellan a free hand to land his army on the peninsula as planned.
So unfolded "one of the spectacular sights of the Civil War," noted
Stephen W. Sears in *George B. McClellan: The Young Napoleon.* In
twenty days a fleet of some 400 vessels "transported 121,500 men,
44 artillery batteries, 1,150 wagons, nearly 15,600 horses and
mules, and a mountain of equipment ranging from pontoon trains
to telegraph wire."

Up the peninsula advanced this great war machine which, in the
end, did prove resistible. McClellan moved through Yorktown and
Williamsburg and then, as the Union army came to within nine
miles of Richmond, Confederate general Joseph Johnston attacked
at Seven Pines on May 31. Severely wounded during the encounter,
Johnston was replaced by Robert E. Lee (McClellan deemed him
"cautious, timid and irresolute"), who took advantage of a cautious,

timid and irresolute pause by McClellan to plan a counter-offensive with the help of troops led by Stonewall Jackson. During McClellan's march up the peninsula toward Richmond, Jackson, with only 16,500 men, had previously managed to divert and pin down in the Shenandoah Valley more than 63,000 Union soldiers. On May 8 Jackson defeated part of the Federal forces in an encounter at McDowell; on May 23 he attacked another Union unit at Front Royal, pursuing it to Winchester where the combatants clashed on May 25; and on June 8 he defeated a third Federal force, finally forcing the Northerners to retreat from the Valley.

On June 17 Jackson left the Shenandoah Valley to join Lee at Richmond. The Seven Days Campaign, which unfolded from June 25 to July 1, included attacks by Lee—reinforced by Jackson after he arrived from the Valley on June 26—on McClellan's positions. This ended McClellan's threat to Richmond and brought the Peninsular Campaign to a close.

Lincoln, frustrated by the failure of McClellan's grandiose plan, now ordered General John Pope, promoted after winning a few easy victories in the West, to attack Richmond from the north. The two armies met on August 29-30 at the Bull Run (Manassas) battlefield, scene of the War's first major encounter in July 1861. As in the First Battle of Bull Run, the South prevailed, with Jackson and Lee joining to defeat Pope, who retreated back to Washington.

Emboldened by his successful defense of Richmond against successive attacks by McClellan and Pope, Lee decided to move the War north. Like Missouri and Kentucky in the western theater, Maryland was a border state, unaligned with the Confederacy but allowing slavery. Hoping to bring Maryland into the South, to relieve Union pressure on Virginia, and to gain recognition of the Confederacy by and help from Europe, Lee entered the border state in early September and occupied Frederick. Before advancing farther into Maryland, Lee sent Jackson to take Harpers Ferry to gain control of that gateway to the Shenandoah Valley. As Jackson captured Harpers Ferry on September 15, McClellan fought through the passes at South Mountain while moving to meet Lee's invasion. To counter a threatened attack by McClellan, Lee (whose original invasion plan a Federal soldier found lying on a road) established his army on the banks of Antietam Creek at Sharpsburg. On September 17 the full force of McClellan's army—some 75,000 men—unleashed an attack on Lee, an assault which resulted in the War's single bloodiest day, with more than 2000 killed and 9000 injured on each side. The ever cautious McClellan refrained from pressing the attack, so permitting Lee to escape unharassed back to Virginia on September 18.

Five days later the War took a new turn on the political front when Lincoln issued the Emancipation Proclamation, granting freedom to all slaves in seceded areas. On the military front, Jeb Stuart led a last feeble Confederate effort in the North when he raided Chambersburg, Pennsylvania, on October 9. In early November Lincoln replaced McClellan with Ambrose E. Burnside, who proposed another campaign to capture Richmond. The plan involved advancing to Fredericksburg, then crossing the Rappahannock River on pontoon bridges and marching on Richmond. When the first Federal troops reached Fredericksburg on November 17, no pontoons had arrived. The delay gave Lee time to fortify the hills above Fredericksburg. By the time the Union men crossed the Rappahannock on December 11, it was too late for an attack but Burnside nevertheless ordered his troops onward—"the maddest enterprise of the War," wrote Fletcher Pratt in *A Short History of the Civil War*—with predictable consequences. After suffering enormous casualties, the Northerners retreated back across the river two days later.

Out in the West in 1862, things went better for the Union, with successes along the waterways and elsewhere which gave the North control of Missouri, Kentucky, the upper Mississippi River and New Orleans. To defend the western section of the Confederacy General Albert Sidney Johnston's 48,000 men were strung out along the 600 miles from the Cumberland Gap to the Mississippi. Northern troops probed for weak points. On January 19-20 a

Union unit defeated a force led by General Felix K. Zollicoffer, who was killed during the encounter, at Mill Springs, Kentucky.

A week later Grant took 15,000 troops through western Kentucky to gain control of the Tennessee and the Cumberland Rivers, defended by Fort Henry and Fort Donelson. On February 6 Fort Henry fell into Grant's hands with little resistance. Grant then pressed on to Fort Donelson, which he took on February 16 after demanding an unconditional surrender. Bruce Catton deemed the fall of Fort Donelson the turning point in the War. Grant's victory, Catton wrote in *U.S. Grant and the American Military Tradition*, "cracked the Confederacy's hold on the West, once and for all." The conquest eventually led to Johnston's abandonment of Nashville; the evacuation of the fortress at Columbus, Kentucky, overlooking the Mississippi; the Northern capture of strategic Island Number 10 in the Mississippi; the occupation of Memphis; and the Northern domination of Kentucky. "In all the war," Catton wrote, "few battles had consequences as far-reaching as this one."

Union victories farther west brought Missouri and northern Arkansas under Union control. On March 7-8 Federal troops held off an assault by Confederate forces at the Battle of Pea Ridge in Arkansas, while between March 3 and April 8 John Pope (later summoned east to lead an attack on Richmond) managed to capture Island Number 10, a strategic spot on the Mississippi between Missouri and Kentucky used by Confederates to block Union boat movements on the waterway.

After taking Fort Donelson, Grant advanced south along the Tennessee River to the village of Pittsburg Landing, about twenty-three miles from Johnston's stronghold at Corinth, Mississippi. Deciding not to wait for Grant to continue on toward his positions, Johnston launched a surprise attack on the Union army at Shiloh on April 6. A Union bullet felled Johnston the first day of the fighting, dominated by the Confederates. The next day, however, Grant, reinforced by Don Carlos Buell, successfully counterattacked, forcing the Southerners to retreat to Corinth, which the Rebels abandoned on May 30 as Union forces approached the city.

At Shiloh—deemed by Charles P. Roland in *An American Iliad: The Story of the Civil War* "the first really great battle of the Civil War"—the casualties amounted to nearly 24,000, the largest loss of any War encounter up to that time. Back in Washington some sensitive citizens abhorred the carnage, and spread the word that the fearless Grant fortified his courage with hearty portions of whisky. To this accusation Lincoln replied, "What brand does he drink? I'd like to send a barrel of the stuff to the other generals."

Not long after Shiloh the Union managed to capture one of the South's leading cities when David G. Farragut took News Orleans on April 29. Farragut boldly led fourteen vessels past Forts Jackson and St. Philip on the lower Mississippi south of New Orleans in the pre-dawn hours of April 24, "The Night the War Was Lost," so Charles L. Dufour titled his book in which he proposes to pinpoint "both the place and the time in the West where the Union Navy won the crucial decision which, three years in advance, pointed the way to Appomattox." Meanwhile, in early June the Union took control of other Mississippi River points farther north in Tennessee—Memphis and Fort Pillow, "almost as soft as its name," wrote Emory M. Thomas in *The American War and Peace* about the flimsy fort. This left Vicksburg as the primary remaining Confederate stronghold on the river.

Federal advances for the most part ended in the West for the rest of 1862. The Confederates, on the other hand, moved on the offensive as they had in the East, with Lee's invasion of Maryland. "Gettysburg [July 1863] is usually referred to as 'the high-water mark of the Confederacy' but the late summer of 1862 is the only period of the war when her armies were advancing victoriously in both the East and the West," noted Joseph B. Mitchell in *Decisive Battles of the Civil War*. In July cavalry raiders John Hunt Morgan and Nathan Bedford Forrest destroyed military supplies and captured Northern troops in forays through Kentucky and Tennessee. In Mississippi General Earl Van Dorn attacked Union General William Rosecrans at Corinth on October 3-4, meeting a successful defense by the North, and on October 8 Confederate general

Braxton Bragg and Buell fought the Battle of Perryville in Kentucky, after which Bragg abandoned the state and returned to Tennessee.

Bragg proceeded to Stones River near Murfreesboro, Tennessee, where on December 31 Rosecrans attacked the Confederates. The Battle of Stones River raged for three days, resulting in 9200 killed and wounded on each side. The encounter ended on January 3, 1863, when Bragg retreated in the direction of Chattanooga. Rosecrans' victory, however, left his army so depleted that his force did not resume the offensive for half a year. But the Confederacy perhaps suffered even more, for "Psychologically, the defeat at Stones River was particularly detrimental to the Southern cause," noted James Lee McDonough in *Stones River—Bloody Winter in Tennessee*. Having lost the first major battle in the Union campaign to seize the Nashville-Chattanooga-Atlanta corridor, the defeat created "a feeling of despair. Was it possible, Southerners wondered, ever to reverse the tide of war?" So ended 1862 in the West.

Activities in the East in 1863 duplicated those of the previous year: a failed Union attempt to defeat Lee at his defensive positions near Richmond, followed by Lee's invasion of the North. In the early part of the year General Joseph Hooker, who had succeeded Burnside as head of the Union army, rebuilt the army, depleted and demoralized by defeats in 1862, to a strength of 134,000 men. Hooker devised a plan to pin Lee down at Fredericksburg while the main Union force approached Richmond from a different direction. After Hooker reached the rail junction of Chancellorsville on April 30, Lee surprised Northerners by dividing his forces, sending most of his men forward to encounter the attackers. Lee then further divided his greatly outnumbered army (57,000 men against Hooker's 105,000) to send Stonewall Jackson on a flanking movement against Hooker. On May 2 Jackson suddenly attacked the Union flank, dealing an overwhelming defeat to the IX Union Corps. That night, however, triumph turned to tragedy for the South when Jackson was accidentally mortally wounded by one of his own men as the general was reconnoitering troop positions to plan a new attack. "That event," wrote Douglas Southall Freeman in *Lee's Lieutenants*, "was regarded in the South after 1865 as equal in fate with secession or the repulse at Gettysburg or loss of Vicksburg." The next day Lee and Jeb Stuart, who had replaced the irreplaceable Jackson, continued the offensive, finally forcing Hooker's men to retreat back across the Rappahannock.

The defeat and retreat stunned the Union. Noah Brooks, a newspaper correspondent for the *Sacramento Union* in Washington during the War, described (in *Washington, D.C. in Lincoln's Time*) Lincoln just after the president had received news of the defeat at Chancellorsville: "I shall never forget that picture of despair. He held a telegram in his hand and...his face, usually sallow, was ashen in hue....The appearance of the president was piteous. Never, as long as I knew him, did he seem to be so broken, so dispirited, and so ghostlike." Realizing that Chancellorsville had shocked and demoralized the enemy, Lee decided to invade the North once again. On June 15 the Southerners crossed the Potomac, then advanced through Maryland and entered Pennsylvania. On June 28 Lincoln replaced Hooker, who failed to intercept Lee, with General George G. Meade.

At the beginning of July the two armies, totalling some 163,000 men, clashed at an obscure town called Gettysburg. In spite of Lee's repeated attacks on the four-mile Federal front—including the famous July 3 "Pickett's Charge," during which General George Pickett lost nearly half of his 15,000 men—the Union lines held, and on July 5 Lee began his retreat back to Virginia. This defeat had much the same effect on the combatants, in the opposite way, as did Lee's victory at Chancellorsville. "While the Battle of Gettysburg could not have been the turning point of a war already lost, the drama of the Confederacy's only successful Army being turned back on its one real invasion exerted a profound effect on the morale of both sides," wrote Clifford Dowdey in *The Land They Fought For*. During the rest of the year Lee and Meade engaged in a series of minor skirmishes and encounters in northern Virginia until December 1, when active operations in the East ended for the winter.

It was in the West, in 1863, where the "war already lost" finally doomed the Confederacy. "The Civil War would not be won or lost on the eastern front," stated James Lee McDonough and James Pickett Jones in *War So Terrible: Sherman and Atlanta.* "There great, bloody battles were waged, the Seven Days, Antietam, Fredericksburg, Chancellorsville, and Gettysburg. Dramatic chapters, which now look larger than life....But after three years of war in the East, no major army had been captured or destroyed by the other side and neither nation's capital had fallen."

The key objective for the Union in the West in 1863 was Vicksburg, the heavily fortified Confederate installation which dominated the Mississippi River in Mississippi. After spending the early part of 1863 digging cutoffs and canals and engaging in other engineering feats—mainly defeats—in various attempts to bypass Vicksburg, Grant finally decided to attack the Southern stronghold directly. On the night of April 30-May 1 he managed to land 16,000 men at Bruinsburg, a hamlet on the east bank of the Mississippi south of Vicksburg. "I was on dry ground on the same side of the river with the enemy," the general recalled in his *Memoirs.* "All the campaigns, labors, hardships and exposures from the month of December...to this time...were for the accomplishment of this one object." After encountering Confederate resistance on his march toward Vicksburg, Grant settled in for a siege of the city, which finally fell on July 4, the day before Lee began to abandon the battlefield at Gettysburg. With simultaneous defeats at those two fateful "burgs"—Vicks and Gettys—the South now faced inevitable decline.

The Union finally controlled the Mississippi River, a long-time objective, an accomplishment Lincoln poetically summarized, "The Father of Waters again goes unvexed to the sea." But Bragg's army continued to vex the North in and near Tennessee, where he and Rosecrans had clashed at the end of 1862 at Stones River. On September 19 the two generals, with about 56,000 men each, again engaged in a bloody battle, this time at Chickamauga in northern Georgia, not far south of Chattanooga. Bragg managed to batter most of the Union forces into disarray, sending them fleeing back to Chattanooga. Only the Northern left flank, under General George H. Thomas (the "Rock of Chickamauga") managed to hold. Although seemingly a great triumph for Bragg, the episode in fact marked the beginning of the end for the South. "In the last analysis, the rock on which [the Confederacy] split was the Rock of Chickamauga," wrote Fletcher Pratt in *A Short History of the Civil War.* "Technically, the battle was a victory; actually it was a defeat, the most crushing, the most decisive any Southern army suffered," for even with superior numbers and positions the Confederates failed to inflict any lasting damage on the Union.

Bragg installed his army atop Lookout Mountain and Missionary Ridge overlooking Chattanooga. Jefferson Davis himself showed up to look down from the commanding heights. Grant, now head of all armies west of the Alleghenies, arrived on the scene and before long he assembled an army of 60,000 soldiers which, from November 23-25, he unleashed to attack the Southern emplacements. In a daring maneuver, Thomas's men scaled Missionary Ridge and overran the enemy's lines, and by November 26 Bragg's army fled south, retreating into Georgia.

This splendid victory inspired Lincoln to appoint Grant commander of all Union armies, with the rank of major general, a grade last held by George Washington. In March 1864 Grant arrived in the East, where "a different kind of war and Robert E. Lee were both waiting," wrote Philip Shaw Paludan in *A People's Contest.* "It would be in the East where Grant's image of tenacity would be tinged with the image of Grant the relentless butcher. And the nation would learn the true costs of unconditional surrender."

Grant's strategy of applying relentless pressure on Lee's defensive line is symbolized by the Union commander's vow: "I propose to fight it out on this line if it takes all summer," a later famous comment the general uttered during his spring 1864 campaign to crush the Confederate army and capture Richmond. The encounter between the two famous generals took on the trappings of high drama: "The contest between Lee and Grant was the greatest civil war spectacle up to that time in either the Old World or the New," claimed Earl Schenck Miers in *The Last Campaign: Grant Saves the Union.*

The Wilderness Campaign which unfolded from May 4, when Grant crossed the Rapidan River, to June 14, when he crossed the James River, consisted of a series of attacks along Lee's front, which extended in a diagonal line some sixty miles southeast from Germanna Ford on the Rapidan to Cold Harbor, ten miles east of Richmond. Grant would attack only to be repulsed by Lee, then the Northerners would slide down the line and attack again. This series of battles at The Wilderness (May 5-7), a thickly wooded area west of Fredericksburg, at Spotsylvania, at Hanover Court House, and at Cold Harbor (June 3) resulted in a loss of about 55,000 Union men and about half that many Confederates. No decisive victory crowned Grant's efforts, but his relentless attacks weakened the Rebels and paved the way for an attempt on Richmond from the south.

On June 15 Grant crossed the James River to march on Petersburg, a key rail center twenty-five miles south of Richmond. Confederate general P.G.T. Beauregard successfully defended Petersburg from June 15 to 18 until Lee arrived with reinforcements, when Grant gave up the attack in favor of a siege. Lee repeated his previously successful strategy—carried out by Stonewall Jackson in the spring of 1862—of trying to divert Grant by manuevers in the Shenandoah Valley, where a series of encounters occurred over the spring and summer. In another diversion, General Jubal Early led Rebel forces through the Valley into Maryland where on July 9 he clashed with Federal forces at the Monocacy River. By July 11, however, he managed to reach Washington, where reinforcements sent by Grant blocked the threat to the capital. On a second excursion into enemy territory, Early burned Chambersburg, Pennsylvania, a deed which so incensed the North that Grant vowed revenge. He ordered General Philip H. Sheridan to ravage the Shenandoah Valley, and after battles near Winchester in mid-September and at Cedar Creek on October 19 the Union gained full control of the Valley. Meanwhile, at Petersburg Grant continued to strengthen his forces as the siege dragged on with little movement; by the end of the year both sides occupied about the same positions as they had five months before.

Out in the West in 1864, William Tecumseh Sherman took command of the army. Grant assigned him to defeat Johnston's Army of Tennessee, which had retreated from Chattanooga to Dalton in northwest Georgia, not far south of the Tennessee line. After Sherman arrived in the area on May 9, Johnston fell back to Resaca where the two armies clashed from May 13 to 16. A similar series of maneuvers unfolded: Sherman advancing south toward Atlanta, Johnston falling back to new positions. On July 7 Johnston was replaced by John Bell Hood, who changed the rhythm of the campaign by proceeding to attack Sherman as the Union forces approached Atlanta, but Sherman pressed on and took the city on September 2.

By November 16, Sherman was ready to leave Atlanta for his devastating march across Georgia to the sea. "Behind us lay Atlanta, smouldering and in ruins, the black smoke riding high in the air and hanging like a pall over the ruined city," Sherman recalled in his *Memoirs*. "We turned our horses' heads to the east; Atlanta was soon lost behind the screen of trees and became a thing of the past. Around it clings many a thought of desperate battle, of hope and fear, that now seem like the memory of a dream." In conformance with his policy of "total war," Sherman inflicted "wholesale destruction," as he put it, as he stormed his way across Georgia to Savannah, which he reached in time to offer the city to Lincoln as a Christmas gift.

The South meanwhile suffered further reverses in Tennessee when Hood's army, escaped from Atlanta, encountered Union forces at Franklin on November 30 and on December 15-16 in Nashville, where the Confederates suffered "the most devastating defeat administered by any army in the whole history of the war," wrote Stanley F. Horn in *The Army of Tennessee.* Hood's shattered army, the only one of the War destroyed on the battlefield, dwindled from 55,000 to fewer than 9000 men. The rout of the Army of Tennessee in effect marked the end of the War in the West.

In the East in 1865 Fort Fisher fell on January 15, so eliminating the defenses for Wilmington, North Carolina, the South's last port. By March Sheridan crushed the last pockets of resistance in the Shenandoah Valley, then he headed east to join Grant at Petersburg. After an attack by Lee on Grant's lines failed, the Union army mounted a full-scale assault on Lee's Petersburg positions at the beginning of April, ending the nine month siege and forcing the Confederates to retreat.

Meanwhile, during the opening months of 1865 Sherman left Savannah and marched on South Carolina, the cradle of the rebellion, which his men "destroyed and wrecked...with a thoroughness and deliberation that arose out of pure hatred for that state," noted John B. Walters in *Merchant of Terror: General Sherman and Total War.* A fragment of Johnston's Army of Tennessee tried to block Sherman's advance across North Carolina in March, but the Confederates were no match for the Union juggernaut and finally surrendered in April.

Grant's assault pressed forward toward Richmond. April 3 "was a quiet night, with its millions of stars. And yet how few could sleep, in anticipation of the entrance of the enemy," noted Richmond resident John B. Jones in *A Rebel War Clerk's Diary.* By the next day Lincoln himself walked the streets of Richmond and sat in the chair occupied only days before by Jefferson Davis. A week later, on April 12, Lee surrendered at Appomattox.

But a more symbolic end to the war, and much else, took place two days later when Union General Robert Anderson raised over Fort Sumter the same flag he had lowered there exactly four years before, on April 14, 1861, at the outbreak of the War. Lincoln had been invited to attend the ceremony but he opted to remain in Washington to tend to official duties. That evening he escaped his cares for a few hours by attending a performance at Ford's Theatre.

Chapter II

Civil War Sites in the Atlantic States

Virginia

Alexandria

Boyhood Home of Robert E. Lee. In 1812 Lee's father, "Light Horse Harry" Lee, brought five year old Robert to this 1795 Federal-style town house where the young man lived until 1825 when he enrolled at West Point.

Christ Church. A silver plaque marks the pew where Lee worshiped. A marker also indicates the communion rail where he was confirmed. In the yard of the church, completed in 1773, Lee was asked to take command of the Army of Northern Virginia.

Fort Ward Museum and Historic Site. At the outbreak of the War, Washington found itself virtually defenseless. The Union began to build a series of earthwork forts known as the Defenses of Washington, and by 1865 a total of one hundred and sixty-two installations guarded the capital, by then one of the Western Hemisphere's most heavily fortified places. Fort Ward—armed with thirty-six guns mounted in five bastions—ranked as the fifth largest of the sixty-eight major Union forts which formed the Defenses network. The museum features a Civil War collection.

Alexandria National Cemetery. The burial ground includes the graves of more than 3,500 Union Soldiers.

Appomattox

Appomattox Court House National Historic Park. At the village the "Lost Cause" was finally lost by the South in April 1865 when Lee surrendered to Ulysses S. Grant. Among the buildings, restored to their 1865 appearance, are the Meeks General Store, the 1819 Clover Hill Tavern, and residences. The surrender took place at the now reconstructed house (the original residence was dismantled in 1893) owned by Wilmer McLean. During the first battle at Manassas—the War's initial major confrontation—a shell dropped down McLean's nearby farmhouse chimney, prompting him to vacate the property and move to Appomattox Court House. The War eventually caught up with McLean there, as Grant and Lee met in his living room for the surrender. According to tradition, McLean commented that "the war began in my front yard and ended in my parlor."

Arlington

Arlington House. For thirty years Lee occupied this magnificent mansion, built by his father-in-law between 1802 and 1818. In his second floor bedroom, on the night of April 19, 1861, Lee pondered his allegiances: for thirty-two years he had served as an officer of the United States Army, but for six generations his family had belonged to Virginia's landed gentry. The next day Lee resigned from the army. Two days later Lee left Arlington House to take command of Virginia's military forces, and never again did the Virginian return to his beloved mansion where he had lived for three decades.

Arlington National Cemetery. The Union army seized Lee's house and land, and in 1864 the North established on the residence grounds a cemetery for Union dead. The burial ground expanded to become the nation's largest national cemetery, with more than 100,000 graves.

Berkeley Plantation. Union General George McClellan

headquartered here in the summer of 1862 during his Peninsular Campaign. President Lincoln visited the estate (where future President William Henry Harrison was born) to confer with McClellan. While stationed at Berkeley in 1862, General Daniel Butterfield composed the later famous bugle call "Taps."

Brandy

The Battle of Brandy Station, the largest cavalry battle in United States history, unfolded at a site now near U.S. highway 15 east of Culpeper. On June 9, 1863, Jeb Stuart's forces—protecting Lee's advance toward Gettysburg—engaged Union troops, an encounter during which Rooney Lee, General Lee's son, suffered wounds.

Buckingham

A mile east of town Lee occupied a tent on the night of April 12, 1865, after his surrender at Appomattox.

Charles City

Evelynton Plantation. In 1847 Edmund Ruffin, Jr., whose father fired the first shot of the War at Fort Sumter, South Carolina, bought the land where he built Evelynton Plantation. Skirmishes took place on the property during the 1862 Peninsular Campaign. Ruffin descendants own the current Georgian Revival-style manor house, built in the 1930s of 250 year old brick.

Charlottesville

A statue in Jackson Park depicts Confederate general Thomas "Stonewall" Jackson mounted on his horse, Little Sorrel, while a monument in Lee Park recalls Lee. The Confederate army established a military hospital in the University of Virginia Rotunda building.

Cumberland Gap

Cumberland Gap National Historic Park includes the famous mountain pass crossed by the Wilderness Road, the main route for westward migration. At the outbreak of the War, the South controlled the strategic Gap, then Union troops captured the pass but evacuated the area three months later. Northern forces later retook the Gap, which they controlled until the end of the War.

Danville

Danville Museum of Fine Arts and History. The museum occupies the Sutherlin House, an 1857 Italian-style villa where for one week, from April 3-10, 1865, Jefferson Davis and the Confederate government made their headquarters. The South's last cabinet meeting took place here on April 4. After the surrender at Appomattox, Davis left Danville and fled farther south.

Fredericksburg

The Fredericksburg and Spotsylvania National Military Park encompasses 8,000 acres where four major battles took place. The South lost some 35,000 men and the North twice as many during the encounters at Fredericksburg, Chancellorsville, the Wilderness and Spotsylvania Court House. The park includes a national cemetery and the house where "Stonewall" Jackson died after accidentally being shot by his own men at Chancellorsville.

Brompton. Now the residence of the president of Mary Washington College, the house perches above the city on Marye's Heights, a Confederate stronghold. The residence still bears signs of damage from two battles. Built in 1740, Brompton stands on land surveyed by George Washington, whose only sister was married to Fielding Lewis, owner of the property.

The National Bank of Fredericksburg. During the War banking operations were removed and the building served as Union headquarters. From the front steps Lincoln addressed soldiers and citizens in 1862. The 1820 structure, restored to its pre-War appearance, is perhaps the nation's oldest building continuously occupied by a bank.

Confederate Cemetery. Nearly 1,500 Southern troops repose at the burial ground.

Front Royal

Warren Rifles Confederate Museum. Items on display include Jackson, Lee and Davis memorabilia.

Warren Heritage Society. The house of Belle Boyd—a Confederate spy who gathered information that helped Jackson win the Battle of Fort Royal—contains a museum which depicts life in the area during the War.

Gordonsville

The Exchange Hotel. Confederates used the Greek Revival-style 1860 railroad hotel as a military hospital. The restored building contains exhibits and antiques.

Hampton

Fort Monroe. Lee was assigned to the fort in 1831 to serve as second in command of the detachment building the facility, which was completed in 1834. Lee's personal knowledge of the fort's strength deterred the Confederacy from attacking the redoubt, which the Union occupied during the War. The Casement Museum includes the cell which held Jefferson Davis after the War. Displays recount the fort's role in the War.

Fort Wood. The fort, started in 1819, occupies an artificial island off the coast near Fort Monroe. Nearby, the ironclad *Monitor* and *Merrimac* clashed on March 9, 1862, in the famous naval battle. Built on Long Island and launched on January 30, 1862, the *Monitor* arrived at Hampton Roads on March 8. When the *Merrimac*—raised in June 1861 after being sunk, then rebuilt as an ironclad vessel—advanced to attack the Union's *Minnesota*, the *Monitor* tried to block the assault. This was the first encounter between ironclad warships. After the Confederates evacuated Norfolk on May 9, the *Merrimac*'s skipper sunk the ship; the *Monitor* was lost in a gale off the coast of Cape Hatteras, North Carolina, on December 31, 1862. Lincoln observed an attempt to capture Norfolk from an observation point at Fort Wood. Cruise boats (804-727-1102) visit the area.

Harrisonburg

Warren-Sipe Museum. The museum houses a twelve foot high electronic relief map, occupying an entire wall and containing more than three hundred lights. Computer operated sequences indicate how Jackson's Valley Campaign unfolded. With less than 17,000 men, the Southern general kept 60,000 Union troops pinned down for twelve weeks.

Lincoln Family Cemetery. Four miles north of town the great-grandparents of Abraham Lincoln repose in the burial ground.

Hopewell

City Point. The peninsula lies at the confluence of the James and the Appomattox Rivers. A cabin built on the grounds of Appomattox Manor, the 1763 home of Dr. Richard Eppes, served as headquarters for Grant, where the general met with Lincoln. Grant's staff used the manor house from June 1864 to March 1865. A number of other surviving structures on the Point also figured in Civil War activities.

Leesburg

Ball's Bluff Civil War Battlefield. At the fourth armed engagement of the War, Confederate soldiers ambushed and killed forty-nine Federal troops. The area includes the nation's smallest national cemetery.

Lexington

Virginia Military Institute. Jackson served as a professor at the school from 1851 to 1861, when he entered the War. The VMI museum includes exhibits on military history from the Mexican War to the Vietnam conflict, with the Civil War featured. One relic is the bullet riddled raincoat Jackson wore when his men shot him by mistake at Chancellorsville.

Jackson House. The only residence Jackson ever owned, which he purchased in 1858, contains a large collection of his personal possessions.

Jackson Grave. Edward Valentine's statue depicts a solemn faced, bearded Jackson, left hand on a sword and right hand holding binoculars.

Washington and Lee University. After the War, Lee became president of Washington College, renamed Washington and Lee following his death in 1870. The Lee Chapel includes his office, the Valentine recumbent statue of the general, and Lee's tomb.

Lynchburg

Fort Early. On June 18, 1864, Confederate general Jubal A. Early repulsed a Union advance in the area. Union general David Hunter's staff included two future presidents: Rutherford B. Hayes and William McKinley. Early reposes at Spring Hill Cemetery in Lynchburg.

City Cemetery. A stone archway in the burial ground leads to the Confederate Cemetery, with 2,000 graves.

Monument Terrace. In the center of downtown a rise honoring soldiers of all wars includes a Confederate soldier bronze statue at the top of the terrace.

Riverside Park. In the park survives the hull of the packet boat *Marshall*, the vessel which carried Jackson's body home to Lexington.

Manassas

Manassas National Battlefield Park. The War's first major battle unfolded here in mid-July 1861, while in late August 1862

Lee's victory at the Second Battle of Manassas opened the way for his invasion of the North. At the dedication of the red sandstone obelisk-like monument in the Confederate Cemetery, where 250 Southern soldiers repose, Lee's son, General W.H.F. Lee, delivered an address. The 5,000 acre park includes trails, viewpoints, explanatory signs and period buildings.

Manassas City Museum. The museum contains Civil War displays, artifacts, weapons and period photos.

Liberia. The 1825 Federal-style plantation manor east of town served from July to September 1861 as Confederate general P.G.T. Beauregard's headquarters. After the First Battle, Jefferson Davis visited the house and here the decision was made not to attack Washington. Liberia later served as headquarters for Union generals McDowell and Sickles, and Lincoln visited the estate. The mansion was perhaps the only house used as headquarters by both armies and visited by both presidents.

Manassas. Through the center of town ran the world's first military railroad, built by the Confederates in the winter of 1861. The track ran from the main line of the Orange and Alexandria (now Norfolk-Southern) to Centreville, six miles northeast, following in general the route of today's highway 28.

Middleburg

Red Fox Inn. Established in 1728 and now believed to be the nation's second oldest operating inn, the Red Fox contains equestrian sculpture and paintings. The building's horse history began during the War when Confederate general Jeb Stuart's cavalry detachment was based at the inn.

Middletown

Belle Grove. James Madison's brother-in-law, Isaac Hite, built this 1794 Federal-style limestone mansion, based in part on a design by Thomas Jefferson. Since 1783 the property has functioned as a working cattle and grain plantation. In the area unfolded the Battle of Cedar Creek, an October 1864 encounter begun when Jubal Early's forces attacked sleeping Union soldiers encamped around Belle Grove. Early's troops routed the Northerners in this early attack, but in the late afternoon General Philip Sheridan—who rode from Winchester through Middletown to the scene of the battle—rallied his men, and the Union forces proceeded to defeat the Confederates. This ensured Union control of the Shenandoah Valley, which remained under Northern domination for the rest of the War. On the attic walls of the house appear the names of Union soldiers.

McDowell

Sitlington's Hill. At the rise on the eastern edge of town occurred the Battle of McDowell, the first engagement of Jackson's Valley Campaign. The house where Jackson spent the night still survives.

Mount Jackson

Confederate Cemetery. This is the only burial ground in Virginia where solely Southern soldiers, and no Yankees, repose.

New Market Battlefield Historic Park

During the Battle of New Market on May 15, 1864, 247 teenage cadets from the Virginia Military Institute at Lexington fought under Confederate general John C. Breckinridge, former vice president of the United States. The Hall of Valor Museum, which presents two films and military exhibits, recalls the campaign and the War.

New Market Battlefield Military Museum. The museum contains displays on all American wars, from the Revolutionary era to the present. Included among the some 1,500 artifacts housed in the building, modeled after Lee's Arlington House, are Civil War items.

Newport News

War Memorial Museum of Virginia. A collection of more than 60,000 military history items includes Civil War displays.

Mariners Museum. Exhibits include Civil War nautical items and material on the famous battle between the ironclads *Monitor* and *Merrimac* in nearby waters. (See the entry for Fort Wood under Hampton.)

Newport News Park. Union trenches, Confederate gun positions and one of the three fortified dams built to create lakes on the Warwick River to block the Northern advance survive in the park.

Orange

St. Thomas Church. The church houses the original pew which Lee used during the winter of 1863. The only surviving example of Thomas Jefferson's church architecture, the 1830s sanctuary includes two Tiffany stained glass windows. While in the area, Lee's army camped on the grounds of Montebello, a mansion where the general and his staff were entertained.

Petersburg

Petersburg National Battlefield. Five rail lines radiated from Petersburg, making the city a key transportation nexus for the Confederacy. From June 1864 to April 1865 Grant mounted a siege which finally brought Petersburg under Union control, followed a week later by Lee's surrender at Appomattox. The siege was the War's longest and involved the conflict's largest battlefield, some 170 square miles. A crater 170 feet by 60 feet, created when Union troops exploded four tons of powder under Confederate positions, remains.

Siege Museum. The attractively proportioned Greek Revival-style Exchange Building houses displays on the ten month siege, with an emphasis on the human side of the War.

Centre Hill Mansion. The house served as Union headquarters after the siege, and—more recently—as the setting for the film *Lincoln* by Gore Vidal.

Farmers Bank. The 1817 building contains a display of Civil War bank notes and the press that printed them.

Old Blandford Church. The 1735 sanctuary was restored in 1901 as a Confederate memorial to honor the 30,000 Southern soldiers buried on the grounds. The church, with fifteen Tiffany stained glass windows, is one of the world's five buildings in which every window was designed by Louis Comfort Tiffany.

Richmond

Museum and White House of the Confederacy. Jefferson Davis and his family occupied the 1818 classic style house from 1861 to 1865. The adjacent museum contains what is believed to be the largest collection of Confederate memorabilia in existence.

Capitol. The Virginia state house, designed by Jefferson, served as the capitol of the Confederacy. Statues and busts of Lee, Jackson and other Southern military heroes decorate the building.

Richmond National Battlefield Park. A nearly 100 mile route takes visitors to ten park units scattered around the city, featuring McClellan's 1862 Peninsular Campaign and Grant's 1864 attacks at Cold Harbor.

St. Paul's Church. Attending services at the church, Davis received word that Federal forces were preparing to invade Richmond.

Monument Avenue. Statues of Confederate leaders stand along the thoroughfare.

American Historical Foundation Museum. Artifacts belonging to Confederate general Jeb Stuart are on display.

Valentine Museum. The studio of sculptor Edward Valentine contains statutes of Civil War figures.

Virginia Historical Society. The Battle Abbey facility contains extensive records, portraits, archives and artifacts relating to the

War. The United Daughters of the Confederacy headquarters is located nearby.

Hollywood Cemetery. Davis, Stuart and other Southern leaders—as well as Presidents James Monroe and John Tyler—repose at the burial ground.

Leight Street Baptist Church. The 1854 Greek Revival-style sanctuary, a building of impressive simplicity, served as a Confederate hospital during the War.

Sailor's (also spelled Saylor's) Creek Battlefield Historical State Park

At the swampy bottomland along Sailor's Creek Lee's army suffered a crushing defeat on April 6, 1865, after fleeing from Petersburg and from Richmond, thirty-five miles northeast. Within three days of this encounter—the War's last major battle—Lee surrendered at Appomattox.

Staunton

The Oaks. Jed Hotchkiss, aide and mapmaker to Lee and Jackson, lived in this house, whose angular three story addition to the front he added in 1888. The Library of Congress contains Hotchkiss's Virginia campaign maps.

Virginia School for the Deaf and Blind. The 1846 Greek Revival-style structure, fronted by six thick columns, served as a hospital during the War.

Strasburg

Strasburg Museum. The former Southern Railway depot houses Civil War relics from area battlefields. During the War era the Manassas Gap Railroad, a spur of the Orange and Alexandria line, passed through Strasburg. When Federal forces blocked or destroyed the main line, Southern soldiers hauled locomotives cross country, then put them on the spur line at Strasburg so the equipment could be sent out to help the Confederate cause else-where.

Burnt Mills. Near where U.S. highway 11 crosses Cedar Creek north of town remain the ruins of two mills, the larger of them (nearest the road) destroyed by Sheridan during his devastating march through the Shenandoah Valley in 1864.

Fisher' Hill. On U.S. 11 two miles south of town rises the hill where Sheridan defeated Early on September 22, 1864.

Banks' Fort. The water tower on a hill west of the town center occupies the site of the fort built, starting May 1862, by Union general Nathaniel P. Banks to house his 10,000 troops.

Stratford

Stratford Hall. Four generations of Lees lived at the 1730s Potomac River plantation, birthplace of Robert E. Lee (1807).

Warrenton

Warren Green Hotel. At the well preserved nineteenth century hostelry, now a county office building, McClellan delivered from the upper porch of the two story arcade his farewell address to officers when the general was relieved of the command of the Army of the Potomac.

Presbyterian and Baptist Churches. The churches on Main Street served as hospitals after both battles of Manasses.

Mosby House. At 173 Main stands the c. 1850 house of Colonel John S. Mosby, who led raids on Warrenton when Federal troops occupied the town.

Williamsburg

College of William and Mary. At the College—90 per cent of whose student body joined the Confederate army—occurred some minor skirmishes. In September 1862 the Wren building suffered fire damage. The same month, Southerners captured thirty-three Union troops as they slept on the college lawn.

Winchester

"Stonewall" Jackson Headquarters Museum. The Confederate general lived in the 1854 Gothic Revival-style house the winter and spring of 1861-2 when he was planning the Shenandoah Valley campaign. The residence—built by Lieutenant Colonel Lewis T. Moore, great-grandfather of actress Mary Tyler Moore —contains a collection of Jackson items and his office, preserved as it appeared during the War.

National Cemetery. At the cemetery repose some 4,500 Union soldiers, killed during the five battles fought in and around Winchester, which changed hands more than seventy times during the War, once four times in a single day. A nearby Confederate cemetery contains the remains of 3,000 Southern troops.

Woodbridge

Leesylvania State Park, opened in 1989, includes remains of gun emplacements on the bluffs overlooking the Potomac. At the site "Light Horse Harry" Lee, father of Robert E. Lee, was born in 1756.

Yorktown

Confederate General J. Bankhead Magruder enlarged the area's 1781 Revolutionary War defenses to block McClellan's thrust up the peninsula toward Richmond. Near Jones Mill Pond survive remains from the 1862 Battle of Williamsburg, while along the James River remain several installations built to prevent the Union navy from advancing up the waterway.

North Carolina

Aberdeen

Bethesda Church. The 1790 sanctuary, near the Malcolm Blue Historical Farm, bears bullet holes from a War battle.

Atlantic Beach

Fort Macon State Park. The 365 acre park includes the fortress, begun in 1826 and completed eight years later, which North Carolina seized from the Federal government at the beginning of the War in 1861. A year later, on April 25, 1862, Union forces heavily bombarded the redoubt, which surrendered the next morning. With the fort's fall, Federal forces controlled the North Carolina coast from Beaufort north to the Virginia line. The North used the installation as a coaling station. After the War it served as a federal prison, and later remained abandoned from 1900 until transferred to North Carolina in 1924, when the area became a state park.

Averasboro

Averasboro Battlefield. At the battleground, near the town of Dunn, occurred on March 16-17, 1865 the first organized resistance to Sherman's thrust into North Carolina. After his "march to the sea" through Georgia, Sherman sent his army of 60,000 men to invade the Carolinas in mid-January 1865. The battle at Averasboro was the prelude to the larger encounter, which took place March 19-25, at Bentonville (see below). Markers and maps around the Averasboro site recall the battle, whose dead repose in Chicora Cemetery. Lebanon, a plantation mansion on the field of battle, served as a hospital. Members of the same family have occupied Lebanon since the picturesque house—topped by a red tin roof and fronted with a two story gallery—was built in the 1840s.

Bentonville Battleground State Historic Site

Union trenches, a Confederate cemetery and the Harper House—furnished as a field hospital—recall the March 1865 battle between Sherman's army and General Joseph E. Johnston's forces, numbering less than half the Union's 60,000 men. The encounter proved to be the last full-scale Confederate offensive action of the

War, as well as the only major attempt to defeat Sherman after his "march to the sea." Although the Confederates initially dominated the action, Union reinforcements eventually forced a retreat, followed on April 26 by Johnston's surrender to Sherman at Bennett Place near Durham (see the Durham entry).

Brunswick Town

In March 1862 the South built Fort Anderson (originally called Fort St. Philips), an activity which revived a settlement moribund for almost a century since the British burned the original town in 1776. Stone and brick salvaged from the burnt town served to build the barracks chimneys of the new fort, constructed to guard the river route leading to Wilmington, an important Southern supply point. After heavy shelling the fort fell to Northern forces on February 19, 1865, a month after nearby Fort Fisher succumbed to Union troops.

Burlington

The Southern General Bed and Breakfast house (919-226-9909) contains antiques and also portraits, books and memorabilia pertaining to Jefferson Davis and Confederate generals. Each of the four guest rooms is based on a theme connected with a Southern general.

Cape Hatteras

The Lighthouse. The present Cape Hatteras lighthouse, which dates from 1869-70, replaced the original 1803 tower located 600 feet north. After the Federal government established the Lighthouse Board in 1852, the Board decided to raise the half-century old tower and to install a newly invented Fresnel lens. Named for its French inventor, the lens used a web of triangular prisms and magnifying glasses to intensify the small oil wick flame into a powerful beacon. During the War, Confederate forces targeted the facility to deprive Union ships of the navigation aide. Union forces successfully defended the tower during a series of skirmishes in 1861, but the Confederates managed to capture and remove the Fresnel lens. The North reactivated the beacon in 1862. After the War, authorities decided it was cheaper to build a new facility than to repair the damaged old lighthouse, which was eventually dynamited and destroyed.

The *Monitor*. The ironclad Union warship survived its famous encounter with the *Merrimac* at Hampton Roads, Virginia, in March 1862, only to succumb to a gale sixteen miles off the coast of Cape Hatteras where the *Monitor* sank on December 31, 1862.

Cashiers

High Hampton Inn resort occupies property used as a summer home for nearly a century by the Hamptons, a prominent South Carolina family. Wade Hampton III served as a Confederate general and as the first governor of South Carolina after Reconstruction.

Chapel Hill

Presbyterian Manse. At the end of the War the house's occupant, Charles Phillips, professor of engineering and mathematics at the University of North Carolina, persuaded Federal troops to spare the school's buildings. The residence, 513 East Franklin Street, was built c.1850 by the Reverend William Mercer Green, who ranked number two in the class of 1818, second only to James K. Polk, future president of the United States.

Lloyd-Wiley House. Cotton mill owner Thomas Lloyd, who served with Lee at Appomattox, lived in the c.1850 house, 412 West Cameron.

Charlotte

Jackson House. "Stonewall" Jackson's wife lived at a house located at 834 West 5th Street during the War.

Mint Museum. The facility, which opened in 1837 as the

nation's first branch mint, served during the War as Confederate headquarters and as a hospital.

Durham

Bennett Place State Historic Site. After the battles at Averasboro and Bentonville failed to stop Sherman's advance, Confederate general Joseph E. Johnston began on April 17, 1865, a series of three meetings with his adversary at the house of James and Nancy Bennitt (as the family spelled the name). At the first meeting Sherman showed Johnston a newly arrived telegram telling of Lincoln's assassination. The generals met again on April 18 and on April 26, when Johnston surrendered nearly 90,000 men in the Carolinas, Georgia and Florida, the largest single troop surrender of the War. In the 1960s the state constructed the present buildings based on the originals, which burned in 1924.

Duke Homestead. During the War soldiers stationed in the Durham area acquired a taste for the bright leaf tobacco cigarettes, a habit which inspired the post-War development of the North Carolina tobacco industry. About the same time as the Confederate surrender at Bennett Place, Washington Duke was released from a Union prison. Penniless, the farmer walked 135 miles to his property, which Federal troops had looted. Duke, then 45, started anew, growing tobacco and then processing it in a log cabin on the farm. So began what became the world's largest tobacco company—an outgrowth of the War—whose origins are recalled by the Duke Homestead.

Fayetteville

Arsenal House. In the closing days of the War Sherman marched into Fayetteville to destroy the Confederate Arsenal. Supposedly as a personal favor for one of his friends, Sherman spared the one story frame house (now the Arts Council office and gallery) across the street.

Cross Creek Cemetery. A Confederate monument commemorates soldiers buried in the graveyard.

Flat Rock

St. John Chapel. Buried at the sanctuary is C.C. Memminger, a banker from Charleston, South Carolina, who from 1861-4 served as the Confederacy's first Secretary of the Treasury. Lincoln biographer Carl Sandburg later occupied Memminger's nearby c.1838 summer house, Connemara. George A. Trenholm, Confederate Treasury Secretary in the last year of the War, also owned a summer house in the area.

Forest City

A house built by James McArthur burned in the mid-1850s, leaving two standing chimneys which inspired the name of the village—Burnt Chimney. During the War the area around the chimneys served as the muster ground for the Burnt Chimney Volunteers, a unit of 125 men which entered the conflict on May 1, 1861. In the 1880s the town changed its name to Forest City.

Guilford College Station

Near the town was born in 1789 Levi Coffin, a leading figure in the Underground Railway, the network of way-stations escaped slaves used to travel north to free territory.

High Point

Oakwood Cemetery. Confederate soldiers repose in the burial ground.

Jamestown

Mendenhall Plantation. The avidly anti-slavery Pennsylvania Quaker Family arrived in the area in the early 1760s, and in 1811 the Mendenhalls started to build the plantation house. Family members served as leaders in the Manumission Society, which favored freeing of the slaves. Under restoration, the property recalls that not all Southern plantation owners supported slavery and the Confederate cause.

Kenansville

"The Liberty Cart." The historical pageant, held from mid-July to late August, includes Civil War scenes. On July 4, 1863, Federal forces destroyed a weapons factory near town which turned out Bowie knives, bayonets and other small arms.

Kinston

The Confederate States Ship *Neuse.* In the fall of 1862 the Confederacy began construction on the Neuse River of the gunboat *Neuse,* one of the twenty-two ironclad ramming vessels built by the South. In March 1863 the ship arrived at Kinston for fitting with engines and other equipment. Low water prevented the craft's entry into the War, so the *Neuse* remained in Kinston. When Union forces advanced along the Neuse River toward Kinston in mid-March 1865 the Confederate commander scuttled the ship to keep it out of Northern hands. The *Neuse* remained under water for nearly a century until completion in 1963 of a local project to raise the relic. A visitor center, built to resemble the top of an ironclad, recounts the story of the C.S.S. *Neuse,* now on display near where the ship was completed in 1864. The *Neuse* is one of only three recovered Civil War ironclads, the others being the C.S.S. *Jackson* at Columbus, Georgia, and the U.S.S. *Cairo* at Vicksburg, Mississippi.

Kure Beach

Fort Fisher State Historic Site. As many as a thousand men labored to build this imposing fortress by the Cape Fear River. Until the last few months of the War, the redoubt served to keep the port of Wilmington open for blockade runners who brought supplies in for the Confederate forces. After the heaviest naval

bombardment of the nineteenth century—some say to that time—
Fort Fisher finally fell to Union forces on January 15, 1865. This
severed the South's last supply line, followed about a month later
by the evacuation of Wilmington, a key supply point. Displays at
the visitor center relate the fort's story, while old earthwork fortifications recall the original installation.

Mocksville

On U.S. highway 64 two miles west of town lies the farm once
owned by Daniel Boone. Hinton Rowan Helper grew up at the
farm house on the property. Helper lived there until shortly before
publishing *The Impending Crisis*, an anti-slavery book which inflamed Southern passions.

Murfreesboro

Rose Bower. Here lived Charles Henry Foster, who in 1859
arrived from Maine to become editor of *The Citizen*, a Union-sym-
pathizing newspaper which so irritated locals that they forced the
Yankee to leave town under the threat of lynching. Foster returned
to Murfreesboro in 1863 as a Union Officer.

Wesleyan Female College. The original cornerstone of the 1853
building marks the site of the school, which Federal troops ransacked, destroying the library and many of the furnishings.

Harrell House. Tristram Capehart—member of the family
which for many years occupied the early nineteenth century residence—advocated an African colony for blacks. Capehart freed
sixty slaves so they could emigrate to Liberia.

Yeates-Vaughn House and Law Office. The office was supposedly built by Jesse Jackson Yeates, a Confederate army officer, three
term United States Congressman, and grandson of Sarah Boone,
Daniel Boone's sister.

New Bern

Charles Slover House. During the War General Ambrose Burnside occupied the brick 1847 townhouse. In 1908 the house was bought by C.D. Bradham, who invented "Brad's Drink," later renamed Pepsi Cola.

Attmore-Oliver House. The New Bern Historical Society occupies the c.1790 residence, which houses a Civil War Museum Room.

Cedar Grove Cemetery. A Confederate monument marks a mass grave in the venerable burial ground, established by Christ Church in 1800 and transferred to the city in 1853.

National Cemetery. The burial ground includes the graves of more than 3,500 Federal troops.

Pettigrew State Park

Near the park—named for area plantation owners—and Lake Phelps lies the Pettigrew family cemetery, where three generations of the clan repose. One family member, serving as a general in the Southern army, led the Confederate charge at Gettysburg.

Somerset Place. Located in the park and by Lake Phelps, the plantation house and out-buildings present a picture of the antebellum way of life. Three hundred slaves maintained the farm, which grew rice and, later, corn. In addition to the surviving structures, archeological work has unearthed the remains of a hospital, chapel and overseer's house.

Plymouth

Federal forces strung a chain across the Roanoke River to defend the city, captured by the Confederates in April 1864 after their armed ship *Albemarle* managed to float over the barrier. Wood from the pews and gallery of Grace Episcopal Church in town served to make coffins for Confederate soldiers.

Raleigh

Mordecai Historic Park. In 1975 the city moved to the park the birthhouse of Andrew Johnson (1808), Lincoln's successor.

North Carolina Museum of History. The museum's more than 100,000 artifacts include War items.

Dorothea Dix Hospital. Opened in 1856 as an insane asylum, the hospital stands on wooded, rolling terrain once part of Theophilus Hunter, Sr.'s eighteenth century plantation. During the Union occupation of Raleigh, Federal troops frequented the grounds.

Oberlin Village. Former slaves established the area after the War. In 1868 the residents of the neighborhood organized a school which pre-dated the advent of Raleigh public grade school by seven years.

Century Post Office. The 1878 building was the first federal project in North Carolina after the War.

Oakwood Cemetery. After Union authorities confiscated the Rock Quarry Cemetery—now the National Cemetery—it became necessary to remove the remains of Southern troops from the burial ground. The Wake County Memorial Association supervised the transfer of 538 bodies to the new Confederate Cemetery, where more than 2,800 Southern soldiers now repose. The seven acre National Cemetery, established in 1866, includes the graves of 1,161 Union soldiers.

Reidsville

In the area Martha D. Martin married in 1847 Stephen A. Douglas, Lincoln's opponent and political adversary in Illinois. She reposes at the Settle family cemetery at Reidsville.

Salisbury

Confederate Monument. The monument dominates the entrance to the downtown area on West Innes Street.

Hall House. The 1820 residence belonged to Dr. Josephus Hall, who served as chief physician at Salisbury's Confederate prison. Stately oaks and boxwoods garnish the grounds of the house, which General George Stoneman, the Union commander, used as his headquarters after the War. Stoneman liberated Salisbury in April 1865, finding miserable conditions at the infamous prison, whose site remains.

Smithfield

Hastings House. The 1854 residence built by William Hastings, a landowner, farmer and merchant, served as a Confederate headquarters for General Joseph E. Johnston.

Boyette Slave House. This relic of the pre-War era is northeast of Smithfield, south of highway 222.

Near Smithfield, on April 12, 1865, Sherman's army celebrated Lee's surrender at Appomattox.

Tarboro

Town Commons. Boston, Massachusetts, and Tarboro boast the nation's only two remaining original town commons. At the six acre public ground, set aside by the town in 1760, stands a monument to Edgecomb County Confederate soldiers.

Topsail Island

Confederates used the area on the coast, south of present-day Marine Corps Camp Lejeune, as a salt source, processing the mineral from ocean waters. Union forces carried out frequent raids on the operation, destroying many of the salt works. During one raid in 1862 the gunboat *Ellis* ran aground in the New River Inlet, at the north end of the island. Confederate forces attacked the ship, which the crew burned before fleeing.

Vance Birthplace

Fifteen miles northeast of Ashville lies the reconstructed birth-house of Zebulon B. Vance, known as the "War Governor of the South." Vance served as governor of North Carolina and as United States Senator for three terms each. The five room log house and six log out-buildings recall the era when Vance rallied the people of North Carolina to the Southern cause. The state provided 125,000 men, one sixth of all Confederate soldiers, and lost more citizens in battle and from disease (a total of 40,000) than any other Southern state.

Warrenton

Bragg House. At the house lived three illustrious Bragg brothers—Confederate general Braxton B., for whom Fort Bragg, near Fayetteville, was named; Thomas B., from 1855-59 governor of North Carolina; and John, a United States Congressman. Their father built Emmanuel Episcopal Church, where on July 5, 1836, *New York Tribune* editor Horace Greeley married.

John White House. White served during the War as North Carolina commissioner to buy ships and supplies in England for the Confederacy. In 1870 Lee stayed at the house while visiting the grave of his daughter, Annie Carter Lee, who spent the early years at an area resort and died in 1862 at age twenty-three.

Weaverville

Dry Ridge Inn. The facility, built in 1849 as the parsonage for the Salem Campground, a religious revival camping area established in 1832, served during the War as a hospital for Confederate soldiers suffering from pneumonia.

Wilmington

Orton Plantation. Established in 1725 as a rice plantation, the property includes Orton House, used by the Union in 1865 as a hospital. Although the house does not receive visitors, it can be seen from the adjacent gardens which are open to the public.

Poplar Grove Historic Plantation. The 1795 peanut plantation recalls the antebellum era and the way of life the South fought to preserve.

MacRae House. Henry Bacon, a one time Wilmington resident who designed the Lincoln Memorial, also designed this 1901 shingle-style residence, 15 South Third Street.

Oakdale Cemetery. Bacon reposes in the burial ground, which also contains the grave of Rose O'Neill Greenhow, who spied for the Confederacy and whose information supposedly prevented Southern forces from being surprised at the First Battle of Manassas in Virginia. The 1852 foliage-filled cemetery also contains a number of other Confederate graves.

Wilmington, the last Confederate Atlantic coast port to remain open to blockade runners, finally surrendered on February 22, 1865, after the fall of Fort Fisher (see Kure Beach). Federal forces spared the town, which thus retains its antebellum flavor.

Williamsboro

In the area of the town, seven miles north of Henderson, lived Varina Howell, Jefferson Davis's second wife.

South Carolina

Abbeville

Burt-Stark House. On May 2, 1865, Jefferson Davis presided at the South's War Council meeting, held at the house, at which the decision was made to disband the Confederate Army. The South thus ended its military effort in the so called "Birthplace of the Confederacy," the name given to Abbeville because the town hosted the first public gathering to consider secession. The assembly voted unanimously on November 22, 1860, that South Carolina should leave the Union.

Trinity Episcopal Church. The sanctuary served as a hospital during the War's final days. In the cemetery repose unknown soldiers killed in the conflict. John Alfred Calhoun, a signer of the Secession Ordinance, is buried here.

Beaufort

John Mark Verdier House. Union forces used the house as headquarters. Beaufort's surrender early in the War—in December 1861—prevented the town's destruction and preserved it as an antebellum enclave. From the front porch of the house the Marquis de Lafayette addressed the townspeople during his 1825 visit.

Maxey House. Also known as the Secession House, the 1813 residence served as the site where South Carolina's Secession Ordinance was written. South Carolina became the first state to secede from the Union, on December 20, 1860.

St. Helena Episcopal Church. The 1724 sanctuary served as a hospital during the War. Surgeons used tombstones, brought inside, as operating tables. Civil War figures repose in the church cemetery.

National Cemetery. The burial ground, established in 1863, includes the graves of 9,000 Union soldiers and 122 Confederates.

Beaufort College. The school, housed in an 1852 building at 800 Carteret, was plundered in 1861 by Union troops, who removed the institution's books and sent them north for sale at auction. Treasury Secretary Salmon P. Chase blocked the sale and the books ended up at the Smithsonian Institution, where most of them burned in a 1868 fire.

Bennetsville

Courthouse. On March 6, 1863 Sherman's forces occupied the Marlboro County courthouse.

Jennings-Brown House. The residence supposedly served as Union headquarters when Federal forces occupied the city.

Bluffton

Secession Oak. The site is where, in 1844, Congressman Robert Barnwell Rhett called for South Carolina to secede.

Boykin's Mill

At the area, nine miles south of Camden, General Edward R. Potter, commanding 2,700 Union troops assigned to destroy the railroad between Sumter and Camden, encountered a small Confederate force on April 19, 1865, in one of the War's last engagements.

Calhoun Mill

The village near Mt. Carmel took its name from the family of Southern statesman John C. Calhoun, born here in 1782. Located seven miles south of Abbesville, the property was settled in the 1750s by Calhoun's father, Patrick.

Camden

Confederate Generals Monument. The fountain includes six columns commemorating the six Southern generals from Camden.

Mulberry Plantation. Here grew up James Chestnut, Jr., a Confederate leader who served as a general and as an assistant to Jefferson Davis. His wife, Mary Boykin Chestnut, wrote a later famous Civil War diary.

Charleston

Fort Sumter National Monument. The War began April 12, 1861, with a Confederate artillery barrage on the outpost, located on a man-made island just off shore from Charleston.

Aiken-Rhett House. Governor William Aiken hosted Jefferson Davis at the 1817 house in 1863. The following year Confederate general P.G.T. Beauregard occupied the house as his headquarters.

Confederate Museum. The museum, established in 1898 by the Daughters of the Confederacy, is housed in the 1841 Market Hall, the main building of the old city market.

St. Philip's Episcopal Church. During the War the congregation donated the church bells—replaced only in 1976—to make cannons. John C. Calhoun is buried in the churchyard.

St. Michael's Episcopal Church. The church bells were melted during the War and sent to England for recasting.

First Scots Presbyterian Church. In 1863 the congregation voted to donate to the Confederacy the sanctuary's bells, never replaced.

Military Museum. The museum includes Civil War exhibits.

The Charleston Museum. The nation's oldest museum, established in 1773, houses Civil War displays.

Magnolia Cemetery. Many Confederate soldiers and South Carolina politicians repose in the graveyard.

Moultrie Tavern. The establishment serves plantation-style cuisine in a War-era ambiance which includes memorabilia of the time.

East Side. After the War more than 3,000 freed slaves, many of them craftsmen and artisans, settled in this neighborhood.

Drayton Hall. The only Ashley River plantation house to survive the War escaped destruction, supposedly because a Confederate officer brought in smallpox-infected slaves whose disease deterred enemy soldiers from entering.

Middleton Place. Sherman's army ransacked and burned the 1755 mansion, but the nation's oldest landscaped garden (1741) survived. In the 1870s and the 1920s the family restored the south wing of the house.

Cheraw

St. David's Episcopal Church. The cemetery contains what is supposedly the nation's oldest monument to Confederate dead. It could not originally refer to Southern troops, as Union forces occupied the area at the time.

Merchant's Bank. The largest bank outside Charleston before the War was the last one to honor Confederate currency. The organization still operates as a bank, but now accepts no Dixie notes—only U.S. greenbacks.

The Lyceum. The 1825 building served as a telegraph and

quartermaster's office during the war. It now houses a town museum.

Inglis-McIver Law Office. J.A. Inglis helped draft South Carolina's Ordinance of Secession.

Chesterfield

In 1865 Union forces burned the seat of Chesterfield County, the state's first county to call for secession. Citizens of the rebuilt town, now an attractive village, assert that the first secession meeting took place at the courthouse, an honor also claimed by Abbeville.

Clemson

Clemson University. The school occupies land given by Thomas G. Clemson, son-in-law of United States senator and vice president John C. Calhoun. On the campus stands the c.1807 Fort Hill, the mansion occupied by Calhoun and by Clemson, who bequeathed his plantation to the state for an agricultural college. The house contains antiques and family mementos.

Columbia

State House. The c. 1855 building bears on the outer western wall six bronze stars marking where Union cannons scored direct hits. The State House grounds contain Confederate monuments, while the interior houses portraits, plaques and statues, some relating to the War era.

Governor's Mansion. Union troops burned all buildings of the Arsenal Academy except the 1855 officers' quarters, later used as a residence for the governor.

University of South Carolina. The World War Memorial Building on the campus houses the Confederate Relic Room, a display of weapons, uniforms, flags and other War items. Federal troops used the area in front of Thomas Cooper Library as a parade ground during the North's military occupation of North Carolina. The soldiers' barracks occupied this and nearby squares. During the War, facilities of South Carolina College (as the school was then called) served as a Confederate hospital and as living quarters for Union soldiers.

Carolina Town House. Sherman established his headquarters here when Federal forces took control of Columbia February 17-19, 1865.

Hampton-Preston Mansion. Wade Hampton III, United States Senator, Confederate general and South Carolina's first post-War governor (1876-9), died at the house in 1902. He reposes in Trinity Episcopal Church, along with two other Wade Hamptons and War-era figures. During the War, one of Sherman's generals occupied the house.

Chestnut Cottage. Mary Boykin Chestnut, author of a later famous War-era diary, lived at the house, where on October 5, 1864, Jefferson Davis and his staff were entertained. From the steps the Confederate president addressed the townspeople.

First Baptist Church. The site of the December 1860 First Secession Convention survived, as Federal troops burned the original 1811 frame church on February 17, 1865, under the mistaken belief that it was there, rather than at the 1859 sanctuary, where the meeting had taken place.

South Carolina State Museum. The museum, which occupies a former textile mill, includes War exhibits.

South Carolina Department of Archives and History. Records as far back as 1731 include War documents. On sale is a facsimile of the state's Ordinance of Secession.

Millwood Plantation. Wade Hampton II built the mansion (before 1820) where Wade Hampton III grew up. Ruins of the historic property, burned by Union troops in 1865, can be seen only on tours offered the last Sunday of the month from March to November (803-252-7742).

West Columbia. On the Salude River stood a four story granite building, burned by Sherman on February 17, 1865, which housed the state's largest cotton factory, operated by slaves. On February

16, the day before entering Columbia, Sherman shelled the capital from batteries in the area of the Congaree River Bridge. The original wooden bridge was burned to delay Sherman's advance.

Darlington

St. James Church. Freedmen established the church in 1866.

Edgefield.

Brooks House. In 1856 United States Congressman Preston Brooks—son of Whitfield Brooks, who built the house in 1815—attacked Senator Charles Sumner of Massachusetts with a cane after he had insulted Senator Andrew P. Butler, Brook's uncle. The incident inflamed public opinion and contributed to events which led to the War.

Holmewood. At the c.1820 house lived Francis Hugh Wardlaw, an author of the December 20, 1860, Ordinance of Secession, by which South Carolina became the first state to secede.

Willowbrook Cemetery. The burial ground includes the graves of 150 Confederate soldiers and the tombs of Preston Brooks and Francis Wardlaw.

Oakley Park. From the balcony of the 1835 mansion speakers incited "Red Shirts" to intimidate blacks from voting, so ensuring the election in 1876 of Wade Hampton III as governor. His victory ended the power of the Reconstructionists.

Mims Corner Store. Confederate general M.C. Butler established the store just after the War. Still in business, the emporium retains the flavor of the era.

Florence

Timrod Park. The memorial to Henry Timrod commemorates the so called Confederate poet laureate, who in 1859 taught at a one room schoolhouse in the area.

Florence was named by William Wallace Harllee, later a Confederate general, for his daughter. During the War, Confederates operated a disease-plagued prison camp in town.

Folly Beach

In 1862 the Confederate army, moving an arms depot from the area, loaded weapons on the steamer *Planter* for shipment elsewhere. Robert Smalls, one of the slave crew, navigated the ship into the hands of Federal forces. Smalls later served as a general and a United States Congressman. At Folly Beach, in the summer of 1934, lived George Gershwin and Dubose Hayward while collaborating on *Porgy and Bess*, the folk opera based on Hayward's novel *Porgy*.

Georgetown

Morgan-Ginsler House. The c.1825 residence served as a hospital for Union officers.

Rainey-Camlin House. Joseph H. Rainey, the first black elected to the United States House (1870), lived in the c.1760 residence.

Prince George Winyah Church. The cemetery includes graves of Confederate soldiers.

Graniteville

At the town operated the South's first cotton mill (1847), considered the place where the region's vast textile business began. Here, then, originated the industry based on the South's antebellum cotton culture and agriculture.

Hartsville

Jacob Kelley House. For two days in 1865 Sherman occupied the c.1820 residence west of town as his headquarters.

Hilton Head

About 13,000 Federal troops—supported by eighteen Union warships and some fifty-five smaller vessels—carried out the nation's largest naval invasion prior to World War II in a November 7, 1861 attack on Fort Walker. On the island the North established the main Atlantic south coast blockade base.

Lancaster

Lancaster Presbyterian Church. When Sherman's army occupied the town his troops stabled their horses in the church, the second oldest brick building in Lancaster County. At the cemetery reposes Dr. Robert Lafayette Crawford, a delegate to the secession convention and Confederate surgeon twice wounded in the War and then killed on April 20, 1863.

Laurens

Andrew Johnson, Lincoln's successor operated in the town a tailor shop with his brother, William.

Laurens City Cemetery. The burial ground contains graves of local War era figures.

Mount Pleasant

Christ Church. East of town stands the brick sanctuary whose interior Union troops destroyed in 1865.

Confederate Cemetery.

Orangeburg

A park now occupies the site of Orangeburg County's third courthouse, built in 1826 and destroyed by Union forces on February 12-13, 1865.

Edisto Gardens. Some 600 soldiers temporarily halted Sherman's advance at the Edisto River Bridge in February 1865. The defenders finally withdrew and retreated to Columbia.

Presbyterian Church. Union soldiers stabled horses in the church basement.

Pendleton

St. Paul's Church. In the churchyard reposes Bernard Elliott Bee, a West Point graduate and Confederate general who on July 21, 1861, at Manassas, Virginia, gave Thomas J. Jackson the nickname "Stonewall." Bee, who commanded a brigade of the Army of the Shenandoah, was mortally wounded the next day. Also buried here is Thomas Green Clemson (died 1888), a native of Philadelphia and one time United States Superintendent of Agriculture, who married John C. Calhoun's daughter, Anna, and later bought the Calhoun home, Fort Hill, at Clemson (see Clemson). The graves of Anna Calhoun Clemson and Mrs. John C. Calhoun are also here.

Pee Dee

Near the bridge over the Great Pee Dee River, about eight miles west of Marion, the Confederates operated a navy yard where in 1863 they built the wooden gunboat C.S.S. *Pee Dee.*

Ridgeland

Pratt Memorial Library. The library includes a collection of Civil War items, as well as other artifacts and books.

Ridgeway

Century House. Confederate general P.G.T. Beauregard made his headquarters at the house on February 17-19, 1865, while he waited to determine Sherman's line of march following the evacuation of Columbia. While here, Beauregard telegraphed Lee telling him that Columbia had been evacuated. Union troops arrived in Ridgeway on February 21.

Rivers Bridge State Park

In 1865 a Georgia Confederate colonel claimed he could defend his position at Rivers Bridge "until next Christmas." With fewer than 1,500 men he managed to delay 22,000 of Sherman's men for two days in early February. Union forces than crossed the Salke-hatchie River and continued on to Columbia. Confederate breast-work fortifications remain to recall the encounter.

Rose Hill State Park

The park includes the restored 1832 plantation mansion of William Henry Gist, an ardent secessionist known as "the Secession Governor." His cousin, States Rights Gist, perished in the War.

Rock Hill

White House. The one time plantation house was used to care for Confederate soldiers during the War. A Confederate monu-ment, removed to Laurelwood Cemetery, once stood in Confeder-ate Park.

Stateburg

Church of the Holy Cross. At the 1850 church near town reposes Revolutionary War hero Thomas Sumter (died 1855), elected to the first United States Congress, whose name designates the Charleston fort where the War began. His name also designates a city and a county.

St. Helena

Penn Normal, Industrial and Agricultural School. The South's first school for freed slaves, established in 1862, occupied St. Helena Baptist Church.

Tombee. The oldest remaining house on the island belonged to Thomas B. Chaplin, whose War-era journal was published under the title *Tombee: Portrait of a Cotton Planter.*

The rather isolated island remains a self-contained enclave some-what reminiscent of the post-War era. Descendants of rice planta-tion slaves continue the black culture which stems from the nineteenth century.

Sullivan's Island

Fort Moultrie. Before the War Sherman served as commanding officer at the fort, a federal military facility from the Revolutionary War until 1947. The present fort—completed in 1809 as the third on the site—now contains a museum relating to seacoast defenses.

Sumter

Battle of Dingle's Mill. At a site 1 1/2 miles south of town on April 9, 1865—the day of Lee's surrender—occurred one of the War's last battles as 158 Southern soldiers managed to block for a few hours the advance of 2,700 Northern troops engaged in destroying area railroads. Sumter native George E. Haynesworth, a cadet at the Citadel in Charleston, fired the first shot on January 9, 1861, at the *Star of the West* in Charleston Harbor.

Winnsboro

Ebenezer A.R. Presbyterian Church. "The Old Brick Church," built in 1788 with bricks hand-molded by congregation members, suffered damage when Federal troops tore out the floors and pews to use rebuilding a bridge across the nearby Little River. On an inside wall of the church a Union soldier wrote an apology for the destruction.

York

Bratton House. At 8 Congress Street stood the 1820s house of Confederate army surgeon Dr. James Rufus Bratton, who bought the property in 1847. On the night of April 27, 1865, Jefferson Davis stayed at the house as he fled south to avoid capture by Federal troops following the fall of Richmond.

Thomas Dixon set his novel *The Clansman*, made into the movie *The Birth of a Nation*, in the York area, where the South Carolina Ku Klux Klan was supposedly founded.

Georgia

Andersonville National Historic Site

The 475 acre park recalls the largest Confederate prison, established in early 1864 after authorities decided to move captured Union soldiers from Richmond to a more secure location with better food supplies. During the camp's fourteen months of operation nearly 13,000 of the 55,000 Union captives there died. The visitors center houses exhibits on the War. The National Cemetery, established in July 1865, contains the graves of 13,669 Union troops, some reinterred there after removal from Confederate burial grounds elsewhere in Georgia.

Andersonville

Drummer Boy Civil War Museum. The museum in town includes a collection of War memorabilia from the North and the South.

The village of Andersonville retains its nineteenth century flavor which recalls when the town served as a prisoner receiving point and as a supply center for the prison.

Athens

City Hall. On the grounds stands the 1862 double-barreled cannon designed to sweep a chain across the battlefield. The Athens Foundry, which cast the cannon, also fabricated the 1859 main gateway arch to the University of Georgia.

University of Georgia. Union soldiers camped on the grounds of the chapel, whose columns they used for target practice. The Ilah Dunlap Little Memorial Library collection includes whiskers snipped off Jefferson Davis's chin.

Taylor-Grady House. Henry Grady lived at the residence when he attended the University. A well known Southern moderate who helped heal the wounds of the War, Grady—known as the voice of the New South—edited the *Atlanta Constitution* from 1879 to 1889.

Atlanta

Cyclorama. The 1885 cylindrical canvas forms part of a multimedia show depicting the July 22, 1864, Battle of Atlanta. Sherman burned the city, a key Confederate rail center, destroying two-thirds of its houses and all of its commercial establishments. The state of Georgia lost three-quarters of its material wealth during the War.

Capitol. Flanking the plaza leading to the main entrance of the state house are metal markers, installed by the United Daughters of the Confederacy, recounting the "Siege of Atlanta," the "Evacuation of Atlanta," the "Battle of Ezra Church," and "The Transfer of Command." During the occupation of Atlanta in 1864, Federal troops camped on the Washington Street side of the capitol grounds, where on September 6, 1864, Union authorities ordered citizens to assemble for registration and eviction from the city.

Atlanta Historical Society. Walter McElreath Hall houses the exhibit "Atlanta and the War: 1861-65."

Georgia Department of Archives and History. The boxy windowless marble building houses a hand-carved mahogany staircase backed by glass windows depicting the rise and fall of the Confederacy. These originally embellished the 1903 castle-like Amos Rhodes residence, now headquarters of the Georgia Trust for Historic Preservation.

Fulton County Library. The downtown facility includes memorabilia of Margaret Mitchell, author of the 1936 War-era saga *Gone with the Wind.*

Oakland Cemetery. Mitchell reposes at the monument-filled Victorian-era cemetery, which also contains the graves of Confederate generals.

McPherson and Monument Avenues. A cannon monument marks the site where Union general James McPherson—who captured Decatur and led the fighting on the eastern side of Atlanta—was killed on July 22, 1864.

Augusta

Confederate Powderworks. The 1862 factory, supposedly the world's largest munitions plant, manufactured more than two million pounds of gunpowder. A 176 foot high obelisk-like chimney survives at what is supposedly the nation's only remaining Confederate-commissioned construction.

Confederate Monument. The 72 foot high marble shaft bears four lifesize statues of Southern generals, but above them stands the likeness of a lowly private, Berry Greenwood Benson, a daring Southern sharpshooter. Local women raised nearly $20,000 for the monument, dedicated in 1878.

Old Slave Market Column. Only the pillar survives at the market, destroyed in 1878 by a cyclone—supposedly as the result of a curse put on the facility by an itinerant preacher.

St. Paul's Church. In the crypt beneath the altar lies the tomb of Leonidas K. Polk, known as the "fighting bishop of the Confederacy."

First Presbyterian Church. The sanctuary was used as a hospital during the War. In 1861 the General Assembly of the Presbyterian Church of the United States held its organizational meeting at the church, designed by Robert Mills, who also designed the Washington Monument.

Blakely

Courthouse Square. On the square stands the last remaining Confederate flagpole, erected in 1861.

Brunswick

Hofwyl-Broadfield Plantation. This estate, north of town, remains as one of the few surviving pre-War coastal rice farms. The property, a typical "low-country plantation," recalls the antebellum agricultural way of life which the South fought to preserve.

Calhoun

Confederate Cemetery. The burial ground includes the graves of some 400 soldiers killed in the 1864 Battle of Resaca.

Cartersville

Cooper's Iron Works. A furnace survives as remnant of the factory which supplied iron to the Confederacy. Sherman destroyed the facility in May 1864.

Stilesboro Academy. The 1859 building housed a sewing center where workers tailored items worn by Confederate soldiers. Students from the Academy served in the Southern army.

Depot. In May 1864 Southern soldiers barricaded themselves inside the building, then opened gunports by removing some of the depot's building blocks.

Roselawn Museum and Etowah Historic Museum. Exhibits at both collections include War items.

Etowah River Bridge. East of town, on the way to Allatoona Pass, survive pillars of the bridge burned by Confederate forces as they retreated on October 5, 1864.

Cassville

Confederate Cemetery. Among the 400 Southern soldiers buried here is General William T. Wofford.

Cave Spring

Baptist Church. The 1851 sanctuary includes a balcony where slaves sat during services.

Chickamauga and Chattanooga National Military Park

The Park, the nation's first (1895) and the largest such facility, includes in the Georgia portion a visitor center with a weapons collection, and a seven mile driving tour through the battlefield. A total of 34,000 Union and Confederate soldiers died during the late 1863 clashes. Sherman's victory opened the way for his devastating advance through Georgia on to the sea.

Gordon-Lee Mansion. The 1847 house served as a Union hospital in 1863.

Clinton

Battles swirled in and around the hamlet, where in November 1864 a unit of Sherman's forces, including 20,000 soldiers and 4,000 head of cattle, camped on the way to Savannah. About a dozen early nineteenth century houses which survived Sherman's destruction recall a pre-War Georgia rural county seat. Union cavalry general Judson Kilpatrick made his headquarters at the 1810 Parrish-Billue House. At the Iverson-Edge House lived the Iverson family, whose father and son both served as Confederate brigadier generals.

Columbus

Naval Museum. The museum houses hulls of the gunboats *Chattaoochee* and *Muscogee*, raised from the Chattahoochee River a century after Southerners sank the vessels to prevent their capture.

Columbus Iron Works. Along the river stands the large former foundry, established in 1853, where the South manufactured cannons.

Fort Benning. The base was named in the late 1920s for the Columbus native Henry L. Benning, a Confederate general.

Dalton

Dug Gap Battle Park. The 2 1/2 acre park includes some 1,200 feet of Confederate breastworks which helped Southerners successfully defend against Union forces ten times as numerous.

Blunt House. The 1848 residence served as a Union hospital in 1864.

Western and Atlantic Depot. The 1850 terminal housed a Confederate ordnance depot.

Confederate Cemetery. The burial ground has 421 Confederate and four Union graves.

Decatur

Decatur Cemetery. One grave belongs to Mary Gay, heroine of the Battle of Decatur and author of *Life in Dixie During the War.* An obelisk of Italian marble—imported during the War by Southern blockade runners—marks the grave of Charles Murphey, delegate to the Secession Convention. Murphey often stated he hoped he would not live to see Georgia secede. He died before the convention began, so Murphey's wish was granted.

Mason's Corner. Opposite Decatur Square to the northwest stood the house of Ezekiel Mason, where women gathered during the War to tailor uniforms for the Dekalb Light Infantry.

Depot. Although dating from 1891, the depot recalls that Decatur served as a way-station to Terminus, Atlanta's original name. The rail line, attracting Federal troops to the area to destroy the tracks, led to the Battle of Decatur.

High House. According to tradition, Sherman watered his horse from a well in the corner of the lot, where the residence stood on a slightly elevated point.

Eatonton

Uncle Remus Museum. The museum, which occupies a log cabin made from old slave houses, recalls the Southern stories and characters native son Joel Chandler Harris created. Exhibits give the flavor of the antebellum plantation way of life.

Fayetteville

Fife House. Believed to be the nation's only unaltered antebellum residence, the facility housed faculty and students of Fayetteville Academy, attended by Scarlett O'Hara of *Gone with the*

Wind. The library in town named for the author Margaret Mitchell contains memorabilia relating to the novel as well as one of the South's largest collections of books on the War. The novelist did research for her famous War-era saga at the courthouse in nearby Jonesboro.

Fitzgerald

Blue and Grey Museum. The museum houses both Union and Confederate War memorabilia. This unusual mixture of displays from both sides originated because Union veterans established the Deep South town, settling here just after the War. At Fitzgerald lived General Jordan Bush, the last Georgia Confederate veteran, who died in 1952 at age 107.

Hinesville

Military Museum. The museum at Fort Stewart includes displays from the War.

Irwinville

Jefferson Davis Memorial Park. Federal troops captured the Confederate president here in May 1865.

Kingston

Confederate Cemetery. At the graveyard took place the first Confederate Memorial Day celebration, held April 1864. The burial ground includes the graves of 250 Confederate and four Union soldiers.

La Fayette

John B. Gordon Hall. In September 1863 Confederate general Braxton Bragg established his headquarters at the 1863 building, where he planned for the Chickamauga campaign.

Macon

Old Cannonball House. The name originated for the 1853 residence after a cannonball fired by General George Stoneman's forces bounced off a column, smashed through a window and landed in the main hallway. The servants quarters behind the house contains a Confederate Museum.

Woodruff House. At the 1830s mansion a ball was held for Winnie Davis, daughter of the Confederate president.

Madison

The antebellum city became known as "the town Sherman refused to burn," for the Northern commander spared the settlement on his march to the sea. Local residents and U.S. Senator Joshua Hill—who opposed Georgia's secession and had known Sherman in Washington—persuaded the Union forces not to burn Madison.

Marietta

Kennesaw Mountain National Battlefield Park. Cannons and earthworks recall the attempt to block Sherman's march to Atlanta in June 1864.

Big Shanty Museum. An old cotton gin houses "The General," a vintage steam engine stolen by Northerners in April 1862. They intended to head north and destroy Confederate supply lines, but the plan failed. The participants, however, received the first Congressional Medals of Honor awarded. Walt Disney's movie, *The Great Locomotive Chase*, featured the episode.

Confederate Cemetery. More than 3,000 Southern soldiers repose at the burial ground, established in 1863 for fatalities from a train wreck at Allatoona Pass.

National Cemetery. Established in 1866, the graveyard includes the tombs of 10,000 Union soldiers.

Battle of Gilgal Church. Original trenches at the twenty acre park recall the June 15-16, 1864, encounter.

Fair Oaks. Confederate general Johnston occupied the 1852 house as his headquarters during the Battle of Kennesaw Mountain.

Kennesaw House. The gang which stole "The General" met at the house the night before the escapade. On July 3, 1864, Sherman made his headquarters at the house.

Milledgeville

Old State Capitol. Now the administration building for the Georgia Military College, the facility recalls that the town served as the state capitol during the War years. The capital remained at Milledgeville from 1803 until 1868, when Atlanta became Georgia's seat of government. The reconstructed Old Governor's Mansion served as the residence for ten Georgia chief executives.

St. Stephen's Church. Union troops stabled horses in the sanctuary.

Newman

Male Academy Museum. The museum, which occupies the 1833 boys' school building, includes War artifacts. During the conflict Newman served as a medical center, with seven hospitals—which treated wounded of both sides—installed in churches and other buildings. Because of the town's medical facilities, Sherman spared Newman, which contains a number of antebellum houses.

Oxford

The town has a Confederate cemetery.

Resaca

Confederate Cemetery. The burial ground originated when two young girls and two former slaves interred two dead soldiers in a flower garden. The girls' father, Colonel John Green, later donated the land for burial of Confederate troops.

Ringgold

Whitman House. During the 1863 Battle of Ringgold Gap, Grant occupied the house. He offered to pay for his stay in Yankee dollars, but the Whitman family refused the U.S. money. At Ringgold Gap, on May 7, 1864, Sherman began his campaign to take Atlanta.

Rome

Noble Machine Shop Lathe. The huge antique (1847) machine, installed by the train depot, bears scars inflicted by sledge hammers Union troops used to smash the equipment when they destroyed the Noble Iron Works, located by the Etowah River, in November 1864.

Myrtle Hill Cemetery. The enclave includes a monument to Confederate women who cared for the wounded, as well as a statue of General Nathan Bedford Forrest, who successfully defended Rome.

Oak Hill. During the May 1864 military encounters in the Rome area Union troops camped on the grounds of the plantation.

First Presbyterian Church. The 1849 sanctuary served as a hospital during the War.

St. Paul African-Methodist-Episcopal Church. Union troops stabled horses in the 1852 sanctuary.

Rosewell

Rosewell Manufacturing Company Mill. On Vickery Creek remain ruins of the 1838 mill, burned by Sherman's forces in July 1864.

Rosewell Presbyterian Church. Union troops used the town's first church, built c.1840, as a hospital during the occupation in July 1864.

Bulloch Hall. The 1840 Greek Revival-style home where Theodore Roosevelt's mother and grandfather lived includes a room with War displays.

Chattahoochee River Bridge. Confederates burned the original covered bridge as they fled from General Garrard's advancing cavalry.

Sandersville

The last official business of the Confederate States Treasury was transacted in the town.

Savannah

Central of Georgia Depot. The War-era terminal, now housing the visitor center, includes displays of historic artifacts.

Green Meldrim House. The 1826 residence served in December 1864 as Sherman's headquarters at the end of his "march to the sea."

Fort Jackson. The installation, on the south bank of the Savannah River, saw service in the War of 1812 and the Civil War. Historical displays relate to Savannah and the coast.

Fort McAllister. The well preserved War redoubt twenty-two miles south of town defended against several naval attacks but finally fell to Sherman in December 1864. The museum contains artifacts.

Fort Pulaski. The installation, fifteen miles east of town, took eighteen years to build. Lee worked for a time as one of the engineers for the construction. On April 11, 1862, the newly developed rifled cannon for the first time defeated a masonry fortress, making such an installation obsolete.

Sea Island

At Hampton Plantation on the island lived in 1838-39 English actress Fanny Kemble, whose *Journal of a Residence on a Georgia Plantation*, published during the War, inspired anti-slavery sentiment in the North and in England.

Sparta

Hotel Lafayette. War refugees took shelter at the hotel in Sparta, a village east of Eatonton.

Christ Church. While occupying the church at Frederica, Union troops nearly destroyed the sanctuary, rebuilt in the 1880s.

Lighthouse. Confederate soldiers built Fort Brown at the site in 1861. The following year they evacuated the area, destroying the fort and the 75 foot high 1810 lighthouse. The present lighthouse was begun two years after the end of the War.

Stone Mountain

Lee, "Stonewall" Jackson and Jefferson Davis are depicted by huge relief carvings—made between 1923 and 1964—on the world's largest single granite mass. The images comprise the world's largest bas relief sculptures. The 3200 acre park also includes a Civil War museum.

Thomson

Depot. A statue of a female in front of the old depot honors Southern women who supported the Confederate cause.

Thomasville

Confederate Prison. A park now occupies the area which included the prison, recalled by a few ditches that formed part of the facility.

Varnell

Prater's Mill. In February 1864 six hundred Union soldiers camped at the 1855 three story grist mill, and two months later some 2,500 Confederate troops set up camp at the site, located east of the Chickamauga battlefield. To the southwest lies Tunnel Hill, a village with an 1849 railroad tunnel controlled by Union forces in February-March 1864 when Sherman headquartered nearby.

Washington

Robert Toombs House. At the residence lived the radical Confederate supporter known as the "Unreconstructed Rebel." Toombs, Confederate Secretary of State and rival of President Jefferson Davis, resigned and returned to his Washington house where he sulked and criticized Davis's conduct of the War. After hostilities ceased, Toombs refused to take an oath of allegiance to the United States, declaring: "I am not loyal to the existing government of the United States and do not wish to be suspected of loyalty."

Washington-Wilkes Historical Museum. Displays installed in the 1830s dwelling include Confederate memorabilia and a Confederate gun collection.

On May 5, 1865, a remnant of the Confederate cabinet met in Washington before dispersing.

Florida

Amelia Island

Fort Clinch State Park. At Florida's northernmost point, the tip of 13 1/2 mile-long Amelia Island, stands Fort Clinch, built of French military-type brickwork. Both Southern and Northern troops occupied the fort during the War. On the first weekend of the month, costumed performers reenact War-era history.

Fernandina Beach. The area served as a slave smuggling point after the United States banned the importation of slaves. Union forces took control of the area in March 1862.

Apalachicola

Trinity Church. The bell of the 1830s church—one of the state's oldest—was melted to make Confederate cannon.

Cedar Key

Island Hotel. The hostelry—seemingly little changed from the War era—housed both Confederate and Union troops during the conflict.

De Funiak Springs

Confederate Monument. The 1871 monument on the court-house lawn was Florida's first memorial commemorating Confederate soldiers.

Fort Jefferson

Out in the Dry Tortugas, some 70 miles west of Key West, lies the massive outpost, started in 1846 and built over the next thirty years. The government never completed the fort, intended to control navigation in the Gulf of Mexico, as the new rifled cannon—introduced during the War—made this type of installation obsolete (see the entry for Fort Pulaski under the Savannah, Georgia, listing). During the War Federal troops occupied the moat-surrounded, six sided fort, whose 40 million hand-made bricks form fifty foot high walls. The fortress, used as a prison for captured deserters, also held Dr. Samuel Mudd, who set the broken leg of Lincoln assassin John Wilkes Booth. Sentenced to lifetime hard labor, Mudd arrived in 1865 but was pardoned four years later for his work in treating yellow fever victims at the prison during the 1867 epidemic.

Gamble Plantation State Historic Site

The mid-1840s mansion, on the sixteen acre site, survives as the oldest house on Florida's west coast. Major Robert Gamble, Jr., built the residence, centerpiece of a 3,500 acre plantation which extended along the Manatee River and produced sugar, molasses, citrus, olives and wild grapes. In 1925 the mansion was designated the Judah P. Benjamin Confederate Memorial to commemorate the episode when the Confederate Secretary of State hid at the house as he fled from the country. As Benjamin escaped from Richmond on April 2, 1865, and headed south, Federal troops mounted a search for the Confederate cabinet member, who had also served as Attorney General and Secretary of War. On May 15 he crossed the Suwannee River in northern Florida, then arrived in the Gamble mansion area on the 20th. A $40,000 price on Benjamin's head brought searchers to the plantation, where he hid while friends chartered a boat for him. On May 23 Benjamin sailed from Sarasota Bay and made his way via Bimini, Nassau, Havana and St. Thomas to London, where he arrived on August 30.

Jacksonville

Kingsley Plantation State Historic Site. On Fort George Island survives the 1792 plantation house, furnished in pre-War style, and rows of dilapidated slave quarters which recall Zephariah Kingsley's business of importing, training and then re-selling slaves. Troops from both sides used Yellow Bluff Fort on Fort George Island, an earthwork on the north bank of the St. Johns River built by Confederates to supplement the batteries at St. Johns Bluff across the river, used by blockade runners during the War.

Mandarin. In 1867 Harriet Beecher Stowe, author of *Uncle Tom's Cabin,* moved to a winter cottage (12447 Mandarin Road) by the St. Johns River. The steamboat company, which ran vessels on the waterway, paid the writer a stipend to sit on her veranda as a tourist attraction when ships passed by.

Key West

Fort Zachery Taylor State Park. Union troops occupied the fort during the War. What is supposedly the nation's largest group of War cannons, as well as a small museum with artifacts and photos, recall the conflict. During the War Key West—supposedly the only Southern city which never flew the Confederate flag—prospered, as cargoes from nearly three hundred captured Confederate blockade-runners were auctioned in the city.

Lake City

Live Oak Cemetery. The burial ground includes the graves of one hundred fifty-one Confederate soldiers killed at the Battle of Olustee.

Madison

Confederate Memorial Park. The enclave which commemorates the Confederacy serves to remind locals that John C. Breckenridge, the Confederate War Secretary, spent a night in the town in 1865 as he fled from the country after Lee's surrender.

Marianna

Confederate Park. A monument commemorates the September 27, 1864,Battle of Marianna.

At Sylvania, north of town, lived War governor John Milton, a descendant of the English poet of that name. He committed suicide on April Fools Day 1865 shortly after stating in his last message to the legislature that "death would be preferable to reunion."

Torreya State Park. Located south of town, the park includes Confederate gun pits.

Natural Bridge Battlefield State Historic Site

On March 6, 1865,Confederate forces carried out a surprise attack and blocked Union troops—who wore hats labeled "To Tallahassee or Hell"—from advancing to the state capital. Southern soldiers included the "Cradle and Grave Company," so called as the unit consisted of young cadets from the West Florida Seminary (later Florida State University) and oldsters of the Gadsen County Grays, a home guards group.

Olustee Battlefield State Historic Site

On February 20, 1864, a Confederate victory blocked Federal troops from advancing into Florida, thus preventing the North from severing interior supply lines and confining Union forces to the coast. A museum recalls the War's biggest Florida battle, in which 10,000 soldiers participated.

Pensacola

Lee Square. In 1891 the town changed the name from Florida Square to honor the Confederate general. A fifty foot high monument contains a duplicate of the figure at an Alexandria, Virginia, monument.

Pensacola Historical Museum. The museum occupies Old Christ Church, the state's oldest remaining church building (1832), used by Union soldiers as a hospital, barracks, prison and military chapel.

Dorr House. Descendants of Maine native Eben Dorr built the house. Dorr branded the hand of a man named Jonathan Walker for stealing slaves, an incident John Greenleaf Whittier recounted in his poem, "The Branded Hand."

St. Michael's Cemetery. Dorr (died 1846) reposes in the burial ground, as does Stephen R. Mallory (died 1873), U.S. Senator and Secretary of the Navy for the Confederacy, who promoted the development of the ironside warship *Merrimac.*

Lee House. A Confederate officer named William Franklin Lee, who lost an arm at the Battle of Chancellorsville, built the house in 1866. It was moved to its present site and restored by the Pensacola board of realtors for its office.

Tivoli High House. The reconstructed structure recalls the 1805 original, occupied by Union forces during the War.

Seville Square. The area was a popular riding place for Union soldiers.

Fort Pickens. Outside town are the remains of the 1834 installation, now part of the Gulf Islands National Seashore. In the opening days of the War the fort, on Santa Rosa Island, exchanged fire with the Confederate stronghold of Fort Barracas on the nearby mainland. According to some sources, the first shots of the War occurred here and not at Fort Sumter at Charleston, South Carolina. By May 1862 Southern forces were forced to evacuate the Pensacola area, which the Northerners then occupied. Fort Pickens was one of four forts in the South to remain under Union control throughout the War (the others in Florida were Fort Taylor at Key West and Fort Jefferson in the Gulf west of Key West, while the fourth was Fort Monroe in Hampton, Virginia).

San Marcos de Apalache State Museum

The 1679 Spanish-built fort was used by Spaniards and then British and French forces before the Confederates occupied the facility during the War. Exhibits at the museum recall the history of the fort, and a trail leads through Confederate earthworks.

St. Augustine

Castillo de San Marcos National Monument. Union forces controlled the fortress.

On June 2, 1865, St. Augustine native Edmund Kirby Smith surrendered at Galveston, Texas, the last Confederate force of the War. When Smith, a West Point graduate, died in 1893 he was the last surviving full general of either side.

Suwannee River State Park

This park contains the remains of a Confederate defensive installation.

Tallahassee

The Grove. From the front steps of the 1836 residence, built by two-time territorial governor Richard Keith Call, the moderate politician delivered a warning in January 1861, just after Florida had seceded, to Southern sympathizers gathered there: "Well, gentlemen, all I wish to say to you is that you have just opened the gates of hell."

White Springs

Stephen Foster Culture Center. A diorama and displays—including memorabilia and manuscripts of the composer—recall the War-era Southern-theme songs written by Foster.

Yulee Sugar Mill State Historic Site

In 1864 Union troops destroyed the sugar plantation, established in 1851 by David Levy Yulee, Florida's first U.S. Senator. Ruins of the operation—which supplied sugar to the Confederate army—remain.

Chapter III

Civil War Sites in the Gulf and the Mississippi States

Alabama

Athens

Founders Hall. The 1842 college building was spared from being burned by Union troops when a local resident produced a letter supposedly written by President Lincoln.

Sulfur Trestle Fort Site. Pesky Confederate general Nathan Bedford Forrest burned the seventy square yard Union outpost, southwest of town, during his raids in northern Alabama to disrupt Federal supply lines. In an experiment designed to free regular troops for front line duty, two companies of black troops—ex-slaves and free blacks—manned the position for the Union.

Auburn

A monument at the railroad station commemorates the occasion when Jefferson Davis, on his way to his inauguration in Montgomery, reviewed local troops on February 16, 1861.

Pine Hill Cemetery. Nearly 100 Confederate soldiers, honored by a monument, repose at the burial ground.

Bessemer

Tannehill Historical State Park. Union troops heavily damaged the furnaces here. One pre-War blast furnace which made iron for the Confederacy has been restored.

Thomas H. Owen House. The house was built in the 1830s by Owen, later a partner in a small forge which supplied iron to the Confederate army.

Bessemer Hall of History. Exhibits at the renovated Southern Railway depot include War artifacts.

Blakeley Park

Historic Blakeley Park, at the site of a town chartered in 1814 and once larger than Mobile, lies on the eastern edge of the Mobile Bay delta near the town of Spanish Fort, so named for the 1798 installation built there. A yellow fever epidemic and a bust after a boom depopulated Blakeley Park, where what was supposedly the War's last battle—after Lee's surrender—took place. *Harper's Weekly* noted in 1865 that "probably the last charge of the war, it was as gallant as any on record." Established as a state park in 1981, and supposedly the largest site east of the Mississippi listed on the National Register, the 3800 acre enclave includes old rifle pits, battery sites, the remains of earthen forts, and breastworks considered among the best preserved of the War.

Bon Secour

On the shores of Bon Secour Bay in Baldwin County at the southeast corner of Mobile Bay stands the Swift-Coles House. Lumber magnate Charles A. Swift built the house, which his heirs sold to Nik Coles, who had often expressed a desire to own the elegant mansion. Local legend relates that a band of cavalrymen known as the "Baldwin Grays" would rally at the house, then sally forth to intercept Union forces engaged in pillaging salt and lumber in Bon Secour.

Cahaba

Now a ghost town with a few fragments of antebellum buildings, Cahaba served as the seat of Dallas County for nearly half a century, until 1866, and as state capital from 1818 to 1825. Yellow fever and area "Blue and Gray" encounters during the War reduced the town to a skeleton. In 1864 the Confederates established a prison in the town.

Citronville

On May 4, 1865 the last Confederate forces east of the Mississippi surrendered here.

Demopolis

Bluff Hall. The family of Francis Strother Lyon, a lawyer and cotton planter who served in both the U.S. and Confederate legislatures, built the house in 1832, adding the portico and back wing in 1850. During the War many Confederate political and military figures visited the mansion, named for the chalk bluff where the house stands above the Tombigbee River. In October 1863 Lyon entertained Jefferson Davis at Bluff Hall, whose other visitors included General Zachary Deas, who married a daughter of Lyon, and General Leonidas Polk, whose son married another Lyon daughter.

Double Springs

The Free State of Winston Festival recalls when Winston County, whose seat is at Double Springs, considering seceding from the Confederate States of America.

Eufaula

Shorter Mansion. The neo-classic-style residence, now a museum, houses Confederate relics.

Florence

Popes Tavern and Museum. The one story structure, constructed by slave labor in 1811, served as a hospital during the War.

Peters Cemetery. A monument decorated with shells and figurines and bearing a reference to the Fourteenth Amendment honors slaves buried in the graveyard.

University of North Alabama. Sherman occupied 1855 Wesleyan Hall as his headquarters while on his way to reinforce Union units in Tennessee.

Fort Morgan

The pentagonal brick fort built between 1819 and 1834 occupies a spit of land at the entrance to Mobile Bay. On January 4, 1861, a week before Alabama seceded, Union forces were ousted from the fort by Confederate soldiers, who occupied the outpost during most of the War. The Southerners strung mines, then called torpedoes, across the channel to block the Union fleet, commanded by Admiral David Farragut, from entering the bay. During the Battle of Mobile Bay on August 4, 1864, guns at the fort damaged the *Tecumseh,* one of Farragut's fleet. As the ship sank, Farragut uttered his later famous war cry, "Damn the torpedoes. Full speed ahead!" The commander of the Confederate fleet, Admiral Franklin Buchanan, surrendered to the Federal navy, and by August 9 Union forces captured nearby Fort Gaines, an outpost on Dauphine Island which guarded the western approach to the bay. Like Fort Morgan, Fort Gaines is a five-sided brick structure; cannons and other relics of the War remain at the fortress. During the night of August 22 the North rained more than 3000 cannonballs onto Fort Morgan, which surrendered the next afternoon. A ferry, which takes cars, travels between Dauphine Island and Fort Morgan.

Gadsden

A bas-relief recalls Emma Sansom, a fifteen year old who guided

Nathan Bedford Forrest when the Confederate raider passed through Gadsden pursuing Federal troops.

Huntsville

At Huntsville lived two major Confederate figures: John Hunt Morgan, the "Thunderbolt of the Confederacy," so called for his lightning-like raids, born at 558 Franklin Street (see also the entry for Lexington, Kentucky), and Leroy Pope Walker, the Secretary of War who issued the orders to fire on Fort Sumter.

Marion

Judson College. By now one of the nation's oldest colleges for women, the school was the successor to the Judson Female Institute, organized in 1838. Nicola Marschall, who taught at the college, designed the Confederate flag. A monument at the Perry County courthouse honors her.

Marion Military Institute. The preparatory school and junior college, a successor to Howard College, established in 1842, maintains various Confederate-type traditions.

Mobile

Admiral Semmes House. Mobile citizens donated the house in 1871 as a residence for Admiral Raphael Semmes. A statue and a waterfront park in town also commemorate the Confederate officer.

Bragg-Mitchell Mansion. John Bragg, judge and U.S. Congressman, built the house in 1855. His brother, the renowned Confederate general Braxton Bragg, once delivered an address from the iron balcony at the house. When the War began Judge Bragg moved the furnishings at the mansion to a plantation house, but Federal troops raided the country estate and burned the possessions Bragg had taken there for safekeeping. During the War Confederate soldiers cut down all the oaks on the grounds of the Bragg Mansion to open fields of fire for artillery. After the War, Judge

Bragg started a new stand of oaks, using acorns he had salvaged from the original trees.

DeTonti Square Historic District. The nine block area just north of the downtown business district survives as Mobile's oldest residential district, with houses dating from the decade before the War. Admiral Franklin Buchanan, Confederate naval officer at the 1864 Battle of Mobile Bay, occupied the third floor of the large three story brick building at 250 St. Anthony Street.

Condé-Charlotte Street. The 1825 structure—built as the city's first official jail and in the 1840s converted into a residence—includes a Confederate Room, furnished as a Southern parlor at the time the War began.

City Museum. The museum, which occupies the 1872 Bernstein-Bush House, includes a War Room with uniforms, documents and weapons, among them Admiral Semmes' sword.

Magnolia National Cemetery. The burial ground, designated a national cemetery in 1866, includes the remains of Union soldiers killed in the April 9, 1865, attack on Fort Blakeley during the capture of Mobile. Also interred there are Confederate general Braxton Bragg and members of the crew of the C.S.S. *Hunley*, the world's first submarine.

Africatown U.S.A. State Park. The nation's first state park devoted to African-American history is at Prichard in eastern Mobile by the Mobile River. Sites in the area recall the *Clotilde*, the last known ship carrying a cargo of slaves to the U.S. At Plateau Cemetery repose many of the vessel's passengers, including Cudjoe Lewis, the last survivor of the last slave ship. A memorial to Lewis stands at the Union Baptist Church across the street.

Montevallo

At Brierfield Ironworks Park, seven miles southwest of town, remain ruins of a wartime iron producing furnace.

Montgomery

First White House of the Confederacy. The 1835 Italianate-style residence (moved from another location) houses antiques and personal possessions which belonged to Jefferson Davis and his wife when they occupied the mansion.

State Capitol. Known to some Southerners as the "Independence Hall of the Southern Confederacy," the 1851 Alabama state house holds many memories of the War years. On February 18, 1861, Davis took the oath of office as president of the Confederacy on the capitol portico. The Confederate States of America was formally established in the Senate chamber on February 4 by the Provisional Confederate Congress, representing seven Southern states. Davis's body lay in state in the former state Supreme Court chamber after his death. Three months after being established in Montgomery the Confederate capital was moved to Richmond, Virginia. A $28 million restoration of the capitol building, begun in 1976, was completed in 1992. On the grounds of the capitol across from the White House stands a memorial to Alabama servicemen who died in the War.

Alabama Archives and History Museum. Military history sections include War displays.

Murphy House. During Reconstruction the Union army occupied the house (now the city Waterworks Board) as headquarters.

St. John's. The Episcopal church retains the Davis family pew.

Other War related areas in Montgomery include the site of the Exchange Hotel, where the first Confederate cabinet met; the Gerald House, where Herman F. Arnold wrote the orchestral score for"Dixie"; the State Chamber of Commerce building, where in 1865 General James Wilson read the Emancipation Proclamation to a crowd of blacks; and the Winter Building, from where Secretary of War Leroy Pope Walker telegraphed to give authority for the shelling of Fort Sumter.

Mountain Creek

Confederate Memorial Park lies east of I-65 between Montgomery and Birmingham. An arch with cut-out white letters indicating "Confederate Cemetery" frames the entrance to this burial ground, one of the few where solely Confederate veterans repose. More than 200 Southern soldiers, and fifteen Confederate wives, are buried in two cemeteries at the site. One stone slab marker memorializes James Wildcat Carter, an Indian medicine man who died at age 105; the inscription describes him as "chief scout Gen. Forrest," referring to the famous Confederate raider, General Nathan Bedford Forrest of Tennessee. A log cabin at the park houses War artifacts as well as documents relating to the Confederate Soldiers Home, which operated in the area until closing in 1939. Although the buildings were razed, near the memorial plaque for the home survive cedar trees planted in the early years of the century by request of a widow, living in the expatriate Southern colony in Brazil, to honor her husband.

Point Clear

The present Grand Hotel, since 1981 a Marriott, opened in 1941 as the third version of the original Grand, constructed in 1847. The current building—centerpiece of the 550 acre resort garnished with moss-draped oak trees—includes heart of pine flooring and framing used in the first hotel. A fire in 1869 and then a hurricane in 1893 destroyed the two previous structures. During the War the nearby Gunnison House—built as part of the resort in the 1850s—served as a hospital for Confederate soldiers wounded at Vicksburg, Mississippi. In 1865 the 21st Alabama Regiment used the hotel grounds as an encampment site. The 1869 fire which destroyed the main hotel building also burned records of soldiers treated at the hospital. Lost were the identities of more than 300 men who were buried in a small plot near the present eighteenth tee of the resort's Azalea Golf Course.

Selma

During the War Selma served as an important military manufacturing center. The Brooke Cannon, a well known weapon, was
developed and cast at the Selma Foundry, while an arsenal in town
produced ammunition for the Confederacy. Shipyards on the
Alabama River at Selma built the armored boat *Tennessee*. Few
remnants of the War era remain, as 9,000 Union troops under
General J.H. Wilson burned and looted Selma in the spring of
1865.

A monument recalls the arsenal, which covered three square
blocks, while another marker indicates the site of the navy yard. At
Old Live Oak Cemetery—filled with moss-draped oaks, dogwood,
azaleas and other plantings—repose Confederate officers.

Tuscaloosa

Gorgas House. On the University of Alabama campus stands the
1829 building, one of the nation's oldest college structures, post-
War residence of General Josiah B. Gorgas, Confederate chief of
ordnance, who served as university president. The house contains
nineteenth century silver and furniture. On the campus are a few
War related markers.

Prewitt Slave Cemetery. War of 1812 veteran John Welsh
Prewitt established the burial ground, where slaves and former
slaves were interred before and after the War.

Tuscumbia

Ivy Green. Helen Keller's grandfather built the house in 1820.
His wife Mary was Lee's second cousin. Captain Arthur Keller, a
Confederate officer, brought his second wife to the house where in
1880 their daughter Helen was born.

St. John's. Federal troops stabled their horses in the Episcopal
church.

Joe Wheeler Plantation

"Fighting" Joe Wheeler served as a Confederate cavalry general and later as a U.S. Congressman and as a major general in the Spanish-American War. He was the only Confederate general later to attain that rank in the U.S. Army. During the Civil War china now on display at the c. 1880 two story frame house was buried for safekeeping.

Mississippi

Aberdeen

Gregg-Hamilton House. The c. 1850 Greek Revival-style residence was the home of Confederate General John Gregg.

A number of antebellum buildings—including 1850 The Magnolias, open for tours—recall the affluent pre-War era when Aberdeen was a prosperous Tombigbee River port.

Biloxi

Beauvoir. Memories of the Confederacy abound at the seaside house occupied by Jefferson Davis in the last years of his life. In 1877, at age sixty-nine, the former president of the Confederacy settled at Beauvoir where he lived until his death in 1889. He spent three years while living there writing the two volume *The Rise and Fall of the Confederate Government.* After Davis died, his widow rejected a $100,000 offer for the property from a hotel developer, instead selling the estate to the Mississippi Confederate Veterans for use as a house for veterans, their families and former slaves. The property, which became a public attraction in 1940, includes a Davis family museum, a Confederate museum installed in the former hospital building, and a veterans' cemetery with more than 700 graves and the Tomb of the Unknown Confederate Soldier.

Fort Massachusetts. Excursion boats leave from the Biloxi area (and other points on the coast) to Ship Island, in the Gulf of

Mexico twelve miles from the mainland. On the island survives the 1860s fort, one of the last masonry coastal fortifications in the U.S. During the War the installation served as a Federal prison, housing both military and civilian captives. One inmate was a woman—a New Orleans housewife who celebrated a Union defeat too ardently by telling her small children to spit on Yankee officers. The fort was started in the 1850s under the initiative of the then U.S Secretary of War—none other than Jefferson Davis. After the War broke out, his army briefly controlled the base, but in December 1861 General Benjamin Butler, the Union commander, took the fort over and named the installation—at which he planned the capture of New Orleans—for his home state.

Lighthouse. The sixty-five foot cast iron 1848 lighthouse, a Biloxi landmark, was painted black in mourning when Lincoln was assassinated.

The house at 1428 West Beach in Biloxi includes a date palm growing in the middle of the front steps and towering over the roof. According to tradition the tree occupies the spot where Father Abram Ryan, a Catholic priest, erected a large cross. Newly ordained at the outbreak of the War, the twenty-three year old Ryan, a staunch Confederate supporter, founded the *Banner of the South* and published a collection of patriotic Confederate poetry which he recited at meetings. Ryan, the so called"Poet of the Confederacy," was a frequent visitor at the Biloxi residence during the years 1870-1883 when he served as pastor of St. Mary's in Mobile, Alabama.

Brice's Crossroads National Battlefield Site

The majority of the 500 War encounters in Mississippi took place in the northern part of the state. One major encounter occurred on June 7, 1864, when Nathan Bedford Forrest's unit of some 3,500 Confederates defeated more than twice as many Northerners. The battle resulted when the Union attempted to bisect the South east of the Mississippi River. To thwart the attempt, Forrest decided to attack Sherman's supply line, a one track railroad line from Nashville to Chattanooga. When the Union tried to block Forrest's advance through northern Mississippi toward the line, the armies clashed at Brice's Crossroads. Graves at Bethany Cemetery, monuments, and also a log cabin museum housing relics from the battle at the town of Baldwyn recall the encounter. (See also the Tupelo entry.)

Canton

Sherman established a headquarters in a tent beneath a venerable tree locals dubbed "Sherman Oak." A monument in town honors freed slaves who served with the Confederacy. The Confederate Cemetery contains graves of fatalities from Shiloh and Corinth.

Columbus

Friendship Cemetery. The burial ground is claimed to be the site of the first Memorial Day, originating on April 25, 1866, when three local women decorated the graves of both Union and Confederate soldiers with flowers. Among those buried here are four Southern generals.

Blewett-Harrison-Lee House. One of the generals buried at Friendship Cemetery was Stephen D. Lee, who lived at this 1847 residence. Lee ordered the first shot at Fort Sumter which began the War. Lee served as the first president of Mississippi A & M, forerunner of Mississippi State University at Starkville, and was commander of the United Confederate Veterans. Now a museum, the house contains nineteenth century memorabilia and period items.

No major battles took place in Columbus, one of the few Mississippi cities never invaded. The town served as a medical center for both armies, with churches converted into hospitals, and the Confederacy operated an arsenal, where more than 1,000 people worked, in Columbus.

After Jackson, the state capital, fell to the North the Mississippi

There are hundreds of historic sites of Civil War interest in Virginia which include exhibits, films, self-guided tours and battle reenactments.

The terrible stone wall. In 1862-1863 some of the bloodiest ground in history was in Fredericksburg.

The Stone House at Manassas was used as a field hospital.

Right: *Though within Virginia boundaries, Fort Monroe never fell to the Confederates.*

Below: *The Petersburg site of the "Dictator" in 1864-1865.*

Left and below: The Richmond Capitol and a view of the Chickahominy.

The Hillsman House was a field hospital at Sayler's Creek.

The South Carolina State House in Columbia and Fort Sumter in Charleston harbor.

The nation's oldest, largest and most visited military park occupies 8,000 acres in the area around Lookout Mountain.

Wilmington was the last Confederate Atlantic coast port to remain open. Today Chandler's Wharf is open daily.

*Fort Jefferson and Olustee Battlefield are historic Civil War sites in the
state of Florida.*

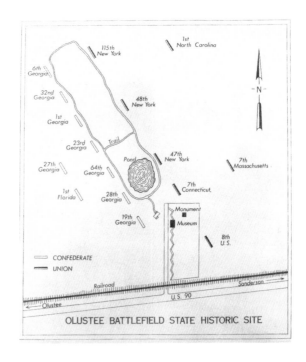

*Civil War memories haunt the huge
Vicksburg National Military Park.*

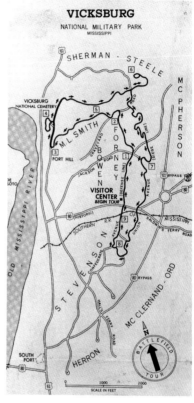

The Perryville, Kentucky, site recalls an October 1862 encounter that was one of the bloodiest.

The cemetery at Stones River was established by an act of Congress in 1862.
There were 23,000 casualties at Shiloh after two days of fighting.

The Elkhorn Tavern was burned during the battle at Pea Ridge, but rebuilt in 1880.

Abraham Lincoln 1860

Lew Wallace

In the Northern states of Illinois and Indiana are many sites that were significant in the lives of men such as Lincoln, Grant and Wallace

Ulysses S. Grant 1865

Burnside Bridge, Sherrick farm and Cornfield Avenue may be toured in Antietam.

Gettysburg Park in Pennsylvania is a delightful place any time of year.

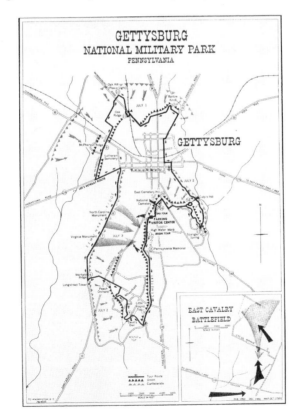

Harpers Ferry can be viewed from Maryland Heights or Shenandoah Street.

legislature met at the Lowndes County courthouse. The roof of First United Methodist Church was ripped off and the metal used to make canteens for Confederate soldiers. According to local lore, Jefferson Davis, while staying at Snowdoun, was roused from slumber and addressed a crowd from the balcony of the house dressed in his nightshirt.

Corinth

National Cemetery. Nearly 6,000 Union soldiers, some two-thirds of them unknown, repose at the twenty acre cemetery, located at the Corinth battlefield.

Battery Robinette. At this installation near downtown the most severe fighting took place, with Federal troops holding off the Southern assault, an attempt in 1862 to recapture the town the Confederates had abandoned the previous May in the face of an approaching Union force of nearly 130,000 men. Many other remnants of the battle—earthworks, rifle pits, battery sites, markers—are scattered around Corinth. One such site is a rifle pit, built by the Confederates in 1862, in an unusual circular design, about fifty feet in diameter.

Curlee House. The c. 1857 residence served as headquarters for various generals, including Confederates Braxton Bragg and Earl Van Dorn and Northerner Henry W. Halleck. Bragg and Halleck also used the building at 709 Jackson Street as a headquarters.

Northeast Mississippi Museum. The museum includes exhibits on and artifacts from the Battle of Corinth.

C. and D. Jarnagin Company in Corinth (601-287-4977) manufactures period uniforms and accessories used by re-enactors of War battles.

Edwards

The Battle of Champion Hill Site, outside of town, recalls the May 16, 1863, encounter, the most fierce of the Vicksburg Campaign and the direct prelude to the fall of Vicksburg. General John

C. Pemberton led 20,000 of the 30,000 Confederate troops entrenched at Vicksburg out to meet Grant's advancing army of 30,000 men. The forces clashed at Champion Hill, a seventy foot ridge named for the nearby Champion family plantation. Pemberton was finally forced to retreat, allowing Grant to continue his advance toward Vicksburg. In the area stand a monument to Confederate general Lloyd Tilghman, killed during the battle, and Coker House, used by both sides as a hospital and as an artillery site.

Ellisville

According to tradition, many Jones County residents—who owned no slaves and resented supporting a "Planters'War"—seceded from the Confederacy, establishing their capital at Ellisville, near Laurel. The "Free State of Jones" citizens raided Confederate and Union supply bases for provisions and terrorized area settlers.

Friars Point

The museum at this remote town, which huddles below the Mississippi River levee, contains some War relics.

At nearby Moon Lake a narrow channel called Yazoo Pass connected the lake with the Mississippi. When Grant sought a way to attack the Confederate stronghold at Vicksburg in 1863 he cut the Yazoo Pass levee and the Mississippi opened a navigation channel across Moon Lake and into the Coldwater River. Grant hoped the new canal would carry him to the Yazoo River so he could attack Vicksburg from behind, but the scheme failed.

Gautier

A few miles north of town David Farragut, in later life the renowned Union admiral, lived as a boy. His father was a justice of the peace for the area.

Grand Gulf Military Monument Park

Confederate forces occupied the strategic area on the Mississippi River to defend Vicksburg, twenty miles north. Unable to take Vicksburg from the west, Grant decided to cross the river downstream. He targeted Grand Gulf as his landing point. Seven ironclad gunboats supported the Union attempt to land at Grand Gulf, but the entrenched Confederates blocked the assault, forcing Grant to move farther south where his forces finally reached the east bank at Bruinsburg. The 400 acre park includes gun emplacements, War artifacts and other reminders of the role Grand Gulf played in Grant's campaign to capture Vicksburg.

Greenwood

The Cottonlandia Museum evokes the agriculture and cotton economy which dominated much of the South in the pre-War era. By 1860, on the eve of the War, America's cotton crop of nearly one billion pounds was some two-thirds of the world's production.

Fort Pemberton. Just west of Cottonlandia lies the site of this make-shift installation, thrown together with cotton bales and logs. In the nearby Tallahatchie River the Confederates sank the captured *Star of the West*—the Union ship fired on at Fort Sumter when War broke out—to block Grant's flotilla of gunboats from proceeding down the Mississippi to Vicksburg in early 1863. Although the *Star* still remains a fallen star, buried in the river, pieces from the boat are on display at Cottonlandia.

Greenwood Cemetery. At the graveyard repose some forty Confederate soldiers from the Battle of Fort Pemberton, including Lieutenant Arza Stoddard, who gave the orders to sink the *Star of the West*.

Grenada

The Grenada Historical Museum includes War relics.
Confederate generals John Pemberton and Sterling Price occu-

pied houses in the town, where the Confederate Cemetery includes the graves of 160 unknown soldiers.

Hattiesburg

The Armed Forces Museum at Camp Shelby, twelve miles south of town, houses almost 2,000 items, from the Mexican War to Vietnam and including Civil War items.

Holly Springs

Holly Springs stood directly in the path of Union attempts to invade Mississippi from the north. The town suffered more than sixty raids by both sides and changed hands so often that residents checked every day to see which flag was flying. Much of the town, however, survived, including sixty or so antebellum houses, many of them evoking War episodes.

The c. 1850 Magnolias' front door bears a scar from a Federal bayonet; 1858 Wakefield belonged to Anne Dickens, who shocked townspeople by marrying a Union officer; 1858 Oakleigh was built by Judge J.W. Clapp, a member of the Confederate Congress who avoided capture by hiding in the capital of one of the mansion's Corinthian columns; Airliewood, occupied by Grant as his head-quarters, suffered when his troops shot all the pickets off the iron fence. Walter Place, occupied by Grant's wife, Julia, fared better. Confederate troops refrained from entering the house while Mrs. Grant resided there. In return, the general put Walter Place off limits to Federal troops for the duration of the War. The house thus safely served as a meeting place for Confederate spies and soldiers.

Other reminders of the War at Holly Springs—"preserved rather than restored," notes one account—include 1837 Hillcrest Cemetery, called "Little Arlington," where thirteen Confederate generals along with other high ranking officers repose; Marshall County Historical Museum, in a former college building, with War items; Van Dorn Avenue, named for General Earl Van Dorn, who on

December 20, 1862, led a successful raid on the town and a Federal supply depot there, which disrupted Grant's planning for the Vicksburg campaign. At Davis Mill, in Benton County just to the east, some 250 Union soldiers defeated some of the Confederate troops after the raid.

Iuka

The Battle of Iuka, fought on September 19, 1862, brought about heavy casualties, including Confederate general Henry Little. Many of the buildings in town served as hospitals. Shady Grove Cemetery includes the graves of some 300 Confederate soldiers; Union men, buried in trenches, were later disinterred for burial at the National Cemetery in Corinth.

Jackson

Old Capitol Museum. The 1838 former statehouse contains historical exhibits, including War displays. History haunts the halls: in 1861 the Ordinance of Secession was passed here; in 1865 delegates assembled for the first Constitutional Convention in the South held after the fall of the Confederacy; in 1884 Jefferson Davis addressed the Mississippi legislature at the capitol.

War Memorial Building. This museum, next to the Old Capitol, includes in a corner room the exhibit "Mississippi in the Confederacy."

Governor's Mansion. At the 1842 mansion—the nation's second oldest continuously occupied governor's mansion and one of only two designated a National Historic Landmark—Sherman hosted a victory dinner after the fall of Vicksburg.

Battlefield Park. Earthworks, trenches, and a remnant of the fortifications built to defend the city survive at the scene of encounters on May 14 and July 9-17, 1863, during the siege of Jackson.

Invaded by Federal forces four times, Jackson was burned by Sherman's men in 1863 and reduced to charred ruins nicknamed

"Chimneyville." At Jackson Sherman supposedly uttered his famous comment, "War is hell."

City Hall. The 1847 structure was one of three public buildings which survived Sherman's burning. Other pre-War buildings include 1857 Manship House, a Gothic Revival cottage occupied by Charles Henry Manship, Jackson's War-time mayor, who surrendered the city to Sherman, and the Oaks, Jackson's oldest house (1846), the residence occupied by Sherman during the 1863 siege. At the Oaks is the sofa from Lincoln's law office in Springfield, Illinois.

Greenwood Cemetery includes Confederate graves.

Lake Washington

St. John's Episcopal Church. Although not damaged by shelling, the church—perched by the lake, located south of Greenville—fell victim to the War. After soldiers removed the windows so the lead frames could be melted down to make bullets, the elements entered the openings and the church eventually decayed.

Laureldale

The Laureldale Springs Confederate Cemetery contains War graves.

Meridian

Merrehope. The twenty room mansion is the only residence, and one of the fewer than a half a dozen buildings, which survived Sherman's February 1864 invasion of Meridian. Confederate general Leonidas Polk occupied the house as a headquarters.

Rose Hill Cemetery. A memorial commemorates Confederate soldiers killed in Meridian during the War. The Marion Confederate Cemetery, on Highway 45 north, also contains War graves.

Mound Bayou

At Davis Bend, on the Mississippi south of Vicksburg, Joseph

Davis and his brother Jefferson, the Confederate president, owned extensive plantations which the Union confiscated during the War. The Freedmen's Bureau established at the properties a model colony run by former slaves. Drought and floods eventually thwarted the project, so Isaiah Montgomery, son of the former leader at the colony, moved north to the Mississippi Delta area and established a new black settlement at Mound Bayou.

Natchez

Surrendering early in the War, Natchez escaped destruction and suffered only occupation by Federal troops. Nearly 500 antebellum structures survive in Natchez. Many of them recall War episodes.

Magnolia Hall. The last major mansion built before the War, the 1858 house was damaged in 1862 by shelling from the Union gunboat *Essex*. A shell from the boat struck a small child named Rosalie Beekman, the only known Natchez resident killed during the War.

Rosalie. The c. 1820 brick house on a bluff overlooking the Mississippi served as Union army headquarters. Grant visited the house.

The Briars. Jefferson Davis married Varina Anne Banks Howell here in February 1845.

Monmouth. A room in the slave quarters at the 1818 mansion houses a collection of War memorabilia, including weapons, maps, flags, and letters of Confederate leaders.

Longwood. Three years after construction began in 1858, the basement and basic structure of the octagonal Moorish-style mansion were completed at a cost of $100,000. When the War broke out, the northern artisans and carpenters abandoned their tools and utensils, which still remain as the fleeing Yankee workmen left them in 1861.

William Harris House. The 1835 residence—the first floor built of brick, the upper level of wood—was constructed by the father of Confederate general Nathaniel Harrison Harris.

Both the Natchez Cemetery and the Natchez National Cemetery contain War graves.

Newton

Markers in town describe the 1863 attack by Union Colonel Benjamin Grierson. More than 100 unknown Confederate soldiers repose at the Doolittle Cemetery north of town.

Okolona

When Nathan Bedford Forrest recaptured the town for the Confederates, his brother Jesse was fatally wounded by Union fire. Some 1000 soldiers lie in the Confederate Cemetery.

Oxford

The University of Mississippi, chartered in 1844, held its first session four years later. The Lyceum survives as the only structure of the five original buildings, but the Old Chapel and the Barnard Observatory date from before the War. Wounded from Shiloh and Corinth were housed in university buildings. A small cemetery near the campus contains graves of Southerners who died at Shiloh. According to local legend, when Northerners occupied Oxford for most of December 1862, Union soldiers rode horses through the university's most elegant buildings. Three stained glass windows in 1889 Ventress Hall portray a mustering of the "Grays," a unit of faculty and students which suffered nearly complete casualties at Gettysburg.

Town Square. Oxford's square—described by local resident William Faulkner in his novels, some of them laced with evocations of the War—is one of the South's quintessential such spaces, with its Confederate soldier statue and the "cotehouse," as residents call the Lafayette County government building.

Lamar House. Lucius Quintus Cincinnatus Lamar, Confederate representative in Europe, lived at the house. He is buried at St. Peter's Cemetery, as is Faulkner.

College Hill Presbyterian Church. North of town, on College Hill Road, stands the antebellum Williamsburg-style church where Faulkner married. Union troops camped on the grounds when Sherman occupied the church as his headquarters in December 1862. The original pews and slave gallery doors in the church remain intact.

Pascagoula

Old Spanish Fort and Museum. The 1718 fort is one of the oldest buildings in the Mississippi Valley. Exhibits at the small museum include War memorabilia.

Pontotoc

The Pontotoc Cemetery includes Confederate graves.

Port Gibson

Grant spared Port Gibson as the town "too beautiful to burn." A driving tour of the area between Port Gibson and the Mississippi River to the west traces the route Grant followed after landing at Bruinsburg to begin his advance to Vicksburg. Markers recount the story of how Grant landed 30,000 men on April 30, 1863, gained a foothold on the eastern side of the Mississippi, then made his way north to capture Vicksburg on July 4.

Raymond

After defeating Confederate defenders near Port Gibson, Grant continued east to Raymond where on May 12, 1863, his forces encountered another Southern unit. The Hinds County courthouse and the St. Mark's Episcopal Church served as hospitals; blood stains on the sanctuary floor recall the wounded ministered to at the church. The Raymond Cemetery contain War graves.

Rodney

Remote Rodney, too small to appear on the official Mississippi highway map, once enjoyed prosperity as a thriving Mississippi River port. A cannonball from shelling by a Union boat disfigures the facade of Rodney Presbyterian Church. Confederate cavalrymen captured Union soldiers attending services in the church on September 15, 1863. A plaque on highway 552 indicates the site of a War encounter.

Sardis

At the 1851 Davis Chapel, built by slave labor, is still a slave gallery. A mass grave in the old cemetery contains the bodies of Union and Confederate dead. A slave gallery also may be seen at the 1842 Fredonia Church, the oldest in Panola County.

Senatobia

The Tate County Heritage Museum includes War items.

Tupelo

Tupelo National Battlefield. At the site the Confederate line formed to attack the Union defensive positions. Monuments, markers and artifacts recall the encounter. Sherman's northern Mississippi campaign focused on a single objective: to protect the rail supply line which brought food and ammunition to his army from Louisville through Nashville and Chattanooga. After the Union defeat at Brice's Cross Roads (see that entry), Sherman issued the order to pursue Forrest "to the death, if it costs 10,000 lives and breaks the Treasury." Federal forces left Memphis and crossed northern Mississippi to undefended Tupelo, which they occupied. On the morning of July 14, 1864, Forrest attacked. The Union repulsed the assault and managed to keep the Mobile and Ohio rail line secure until Sherman advanced past Atlanta and thus beyond the line. Although important, the encounters at Brice's Cross Roads and Tupelo were peripheral to Sherman's main campaign in the West and to Grant's clash with Lee in the East.

Lincoln, recalling his rabbit hunting days, said of the side battles, "Those not skinning can hold a leg."

The Tupelo Museum houses artifacts from the Battle of Tupelo and a diorama of the battlefield.

Confederate Grave Sites. The thirteen unknown soldiers buried at the site, just off the Natchez Trace Parkway, were supposedly executed by General Braxton Bragg, their own commander, for various offenses.

Union

Boler's Inn. Built in 1835, the inn was one of the original stops on the stage coach line between Jackson, Mississippi, and Mobile, Alabama. In February 1864 Sherman spent the night here.

Vicksburg

Vicksburg National Military Park. A sixteen mile driving tour leads through the monument-filled battlefields, where trenches, earthworks and cannons indicate Confederate defensive positions. The visitor center contains exhibits on and artifacts from the forty-seven day Siege of Vicksburg. The park's northern section includes the U.S.S. *Cairo* gunboat, salvaged after a century under water. Artifacts from the boat evoke daily life in 1863. At the cemetery in the park three-quarters of the 17,000 graves bear the marking "Unknown." A lesser known burial area in town is the Soldiers Rest Confederate Cemetery on Sky Farm Avenue.

Old Court House Museum. War history haunts the 1858 building. Jefferson Davis—a resident of Warren County when he served as U.S. senator from Mississippi—launched his political career on the grounds, and from the tower Confederate generals observed the 1862 attack on Vicksburg. When Union prisoners were moved into the court room, Federal shelling of the building ceased. Northern troops raised the Stars and Stripes at the courthouse on July 4, 1863, and for more than a century thereafter citizens of Vicksburg refused to celebrate Independence Day. Exhibits at the museum include War memorabilia, Grant's chair, the tie Davis wore when inaugurated Confederate president, and many other era artifacts.

Antebellum mansions. War incidents occurred at many of Vicksburg's early-day houses. At McRaven, Confederates camped in the garden and as late as the 1950s a bomb squad removed a live shell from a wall. Balfour, Union headquarters after the city fell, was the home of War diarist Emma Balfour and site of the 1862 Christmas ball interrupted by news of Union gunboats on the Mississippi. Duff Green housed a hospital. Davis spoke from the balcony of Anchuca. A Union cannonball remains embedded in a wall at Cedar Grove. The 1840s Willis-Cowan House served as headquarters for Confederate general John Pemberton during the siege.

"The Vanishing Glory." The thirty minute multi-media presentation dramatizes the campaign for and siege of Vicksburg.

Toys and Soldiers Museum. Displays include not only miniature soldiers but also War shells and other artifacts.

Christ Church. During the siege, daily services were held at the c. 1839 church, the oldest remaining public building in Vicksburg, in spite of heavy shelling.

Washington

Jefferson College. Jefferson Davis studied at the school, occupied by Union forces during the War.

West Point

Lenoir Plantation. Both Confederate and Union soldiers occupied the 1847 mansion, built by slave labor and located on a 2,000 acre property.

Winona

More than two dozen antebellum houses within a few square blocks give the town a pre-War flavor. At the corner of Carrollton and Church Streets towers the oak under which Jefferson Davis addressed the townspeople.

Woodville

Rosemont Plantation. The parents of Jefferson Davis built the house, which contains many original furnishings, about 1810. Davis family members occupied the residence for eighty-five years. Jefferson, the youngest of ten children, was brought here at age two when the family moved from Kentucky. Five generations of the Davis clan repose at the cemetery.

Yazoo City

Triangle Cultural Center. The Yazoo Historical Museum at the Center includes War artifacts and a scale model of the ironclad ram *Arkansas*, built at the Confederate naval yard, its site indicated by a marker near the Yazoo River. The *Arkansas* helped fend off a July 1862 attack on Vicksburg by David Farragut. Yazoo City native Lieutenant Savvy Read, who served on the *Arkansas,* later helped capture a Union boat by using a wooden log painted to resemble a cannon. On the grounds of the Center stands a 1906 monument honoring the role of Mississippi women during the War. This is supposedly one of only two known memorials which commemorate women of the Confederacy.

Woodbine Mansion. The 1840s house, near Bentonia to the south of Yazoo City, boasts ghosts—so says local legend—including a spirited young woman who gazes out of the east window looking for her beau who never returned from the War. On one glass pane appear the young lovers' initials she scratched in the glass with her engagement ring.

Louisiana

Alexandria

Rosalie Sugar Mill. Union troops spared this c. 1852 house, south of town on Louisiana highway 1208-A off U.S. 71, as the owner was a friend of Sherman.

Pineville National Cemetery includes a monument to 1537 Union soldiers buried at the graveyard.

Bastorp

The Snyder Museum and Creative Art Center contains exhibits on the War and Reconstruction.

Baton Rouge

Old State Capitol. In January 1861 the Secession Convention met in the 1849 statehouse and voted for Louisiana to leave the Union. During the War Union soldiers used the building as a barracks and, briefly, as a prison for Confederate captives. On December 28, 1862, a fire caused by grease which overheated when soldiers prepared supper gutted the capitol, later rebuilt and re-opened in May 1882.

Pentagon Barracks. Confederate forces occupied the 1824 military facility until Federal troops entered Baton Rouge in the summer of 1862 to begin an occupation which lasted until 1879.

Louisiana State University. In the late 1850s none other than William Tecumseh Sherman, later the famous Union general, served as president of the Seminary of Learning, the early name for the institution which became L.S.U. All the students and teachers at the seminary joined the Confederate army, except for one who opted for the Union army and two who remained unaffiliated.

Mount Hope Plantation. Confederate troops used the property to rest and water their horses. A small War museum in the 1817 Creole-style house recalls the era.

Cemeteries. At the National Cemetery repose some 2,000 Union soldiers, and at Magnolia Cemetery occurred the August 1864 Battle of Baton Rouge. A monument at 330 South 19th Street marks the site of an August 5, 1862, battle, during which Confederate lieutenant Alexander H. Todd, Mary Todd Lincoln's half-brother, was killed.

West of the Mississippi lies Port Allen, named for General Henry W. Allen, based in Opelousas as governor of the Confederate part of Louisiana in 1864-5. Allen survived wounds he suffered during the Battle of Baton Rouge. His statue stands in front of the courthouse, while a monument on the grounds of the Old State Capitol (back on the east side of the river) marks Allen's grave site. Also west of the river is the West Baton Rouge Museum, with historical exhibits, including a reconstructed original slave cabin from Allendale Plantation, Allen's property, which was burned during the War.

Beggs

On the grounds of 1829 Homeplace (open to visitors) is the grave of an unknown Confederate soldier.

Belle Chasse

Bellechasse (spelled as one word) Plantation, established in 1808, was acquired in 1844 by Judah P. Benjamin, U.S. senator in the 1850s and later a member of the Confederate cabinet who served as Secretary of State, Secretary of War and Attorney General. After the War Benjamin fled to London where he established a new career as a leading member of the English bar. At the site of the now vanished plantation stands its 1848 bell, to which Benjamin— "to sweeten its tone"—added 200 silver dollars when the molten metal for the bell was being prepared.

Burnside

Houmas House. One of the famous antebellum plantation houses along the Mississippi, 1840 Houmas enjoyed a better fate during the War than many of the neighboring properties. When Union general Benjamin Butler arrived to occupy the plantation, owner John Burnside, an Irishman, argued that as a British subject his holdings should remain exempt from control by the U.S. Butler agreed, and withdrew, and the plantation was spared.

The Cabin Restaurant. The eatery occupies one of ten original slave houses, built a century and a half ago as part of the Monroe Plantation. Newspaper wall coverings to insulate the cabin, slave tools and other relics on display recall the pre-War era. Behind the main cabin stretches a two room slave dwelling from the Welham Plantation.

Cheneyville

Loyd Hall House. The residence, located outside town, was occupied by both Confederate and Union troops. A Union soldier is buried under the house.

Trinity Episcopal Church. The 1820s sanctuary retains its slave gallery and original furnishings.

Chopin

Much of the land in and around Chopin now comprises the 6,000 acre Little Eva Plantation, claimed to be the setting of Harriet Beecher Stowe's famous anti-slavery novel, *Uncle Tom's Cabin.* Local legend has it that plantation owner Robert B. McAlpin, portrayed in the book as Simon Legree, bought Uncle Tom at a sale in New Orleans and brought the slave back to the property. On the grounds stands a ramshackle shack of weathered wood, a replica of the original Uncle Tom's Cabin removed for display at the 1893 Chicago Exposition. A half mile or so beyond the cabin metal markers indicate the graves of McAlpin and "of the person said to be the character portrayed as Uncle Tom." (See the entry for Owensboro, Kentucky, which also claims Uncle Tom was a local character.)

Clinton

Clinton Confederate State Commemorative Area. The four acre cemetery contains the remains of some 150 Southern soldiers, about half of whom perished during the 1863 siege at Port Hudson. The Marston House and Silliman College in town both served as hospitals, which received the sick and wounded from nearby Port Hudson.

Delta

At various places in Mississippi (see the entry for Friars Point) and Louisiana (see the entry for Lake Providence) north of Vicksburg, Grant tried to devise a workable plan to by-pass that Confederate stronghold overlooking the Mississippi. At Delta, Grant dug a canal to change the river's course, an operation he also attempted at De Soto Point, opposite Vicksburg just to the north. None of Grant's schemes worked, so finally he crossed the Mississippi to Bruinsburg, south of Vicksburg.

Derry

Magnolia Plantation. The now restored brick mansion house at this working cotton plantation, dating from 1753, was burned during the War.

Destrehan Plantation

Believed to be the oldest plantation house in the Lower Mississippi Valley, the 1787 property was seized by Union forces and turned into a Freedmen's Colony where newly liberated slaves took training in the economics of agriculture. More than 900 black freedmen were trained at Destrehan, returned after the War to its owners.

Donaldsonville

Northerners destroyed much of the town during the War, especially when they bombarded and burned Donaldsonville in

1862. The c. 1850 building on Railroad Avenue, now occupied by Ferris's Grocery, was used as a headquarters during the War. At nearby Port Barrow lurked guerrilla bands which harassed Federal troops after the occupation of New Orleans. In February 1863 the Union installed a log fort, attacked four months later by a small group of Confederates who captured the outpost. Union gunboats then shelled the Rebels, who soon retreated.

Fort Jackson

Built between 1822 to 1832 to protect the Lower Mississippi and New Orleans, the fort seemingly blocked a river approach to the city from the south. Military strategists believed that wooden ships would find it impossible to pass the fort, which bristled with armaments. In April 1862 Admiral David Farragut brought up the Mississippi a Federal fleet of twenty-four wooden gunboats and nineteen mortar schooners, which unleashed a four day bombardment on Fort Jackson and Fort St. Philip, located nearby on the east bank of the river. On the fifth day seventeen vessels managed to slip past the forts, and after a spirited encounter with Confederate gunboats and rams, the Union boats proceeded north toward New Orleans. Fort Jackson finally surrendered on April 28.

Fort Pike

At the outbreak of the War the Louisiana Militia captured the fort—built at the eastern edge of Lake Pontchartrain between 1818 and 1827—and held it until Federal forces took New Orleans on May 1, 1862. The Union occupied the fort as a base to protect New Orleans and for raids along the Gulf Coast. The Citadel, which the Confederates burned before their retreat, now houses historical exhibits.

Franklin

St. Mary's Parish Museum. Exhibits at the museum, which occupies the c. 1851 Grevemberg House, include War relics. In the spring of 1863 Confederate troops fought a delaying action against Union forces at Franklin.

Geismar

A few miles from town stands Belle Hélène, built in 1841 by Duncan F. Kenner and then named Ashland after Henry Clay's mansion in Lexington, Kentucky (see the entry for Ashland under that city). Jefferson Davis appointed Kenner Confederate minister plenipotentiary to Europe. After the War Federal authorities confiscated the property, which Kenner later recovered.

Grand Coteau

Academy of the Sacred Heart. The world's oldest Society of the Sacred Heart School (1821), the institution escaped damage during the War when General Nathaniel Banks, commander of the 20,000 Federal troops based in Grand Coteau in 1863, placed the school under his protection. At the time, his daughter was attending a Sacred Heart Academy in New York. Archives at the Academy include War era documents.

Hahnville

The town took its name from Michael Hahn, Union governor of Louisiana when the North occupied part of the state in 1864, after which Louisiana had two governors.

Near town lies the site of the old Fashion Plantation, owned by Confederate general Richard Taylor, son of President Zachary Taylor. A skirmish occurred on the property in August 1862 when Union troops defeated an attempt by Confederate forces to take cattle, horses, sheep, mules and slaves from the plantation.

Harrisonburg

Fort Beauregard. Now a park and amphitheater, the site—a natural formation of hills and ravines overlooking the downtown area—served as a Confederate stronghold established in 1862 to block Federal gunboats from ascending the Ouachita River.

Harrisonburg Methodist Church. Bullet holes from the War pock the walls of the church, frequented by soldiers for services.

Catahoula Parish Museum of Natural History. Installed in the courthouse, the museum includes War relics from area encounters.

Innis

On Louisiana highway 418 near Innis, on the grounds of St. Stephens Episcopal Church, stands a statue of a soldier, claimed to be the only monument in the South to an unknown soldier of the War (but see the entry for Beauvoir in Biloxi, Mississippi).

Jackson

Jackson Confederate State Commemorative Area. Although the cemetery here has no marked graves, the one acre site was established during the War to bury soldiers killed in an encounter at nearby Thompson's Creek. Adjacent to the burial ground is Centenary State Commemorative Area, with buildings from Centenary College, a Methodist school. Union troops occupied the Main Academic Building as a headquarters, while the school dorms served as a hospital.

Milbank. Union soldiers enjoyed especially lavish accommodations when they occupied as a barracks the elegant Milbank mansion, fronted by six thirty foot tall columns and a two level veranda.

Lake Providence

In the center of town remain traces of the canal Grant dug in a effort to allow Union gunboats to leave the Mississippi and, on a network of rivers and bayous, to bypass the heavily fortified bluffs at Vicksburg, Mississippi, downstream. (See also the entry for Delta, Louisiana.)

Grant supposedly stayed at 1841 Arlington, outside town. Union generals MacPherson, McMillan and MacArthur did use the house as a headquarters.

Lafayette

At the corner of Jefferson and Lee Streets stands a 1922 statue of Confederate general Alfred Mouton, son of Louisiana's first Cajun governor. Mouton lived in the nearby residence now housing the Lafayette Museum, which contains War items. He was killed at Mansfield (see the Mansfield State Commemorative Area entry) on April 8, 1864, and is buried in Lafayette.

Cathedral of St. John the Evangelist. During the War Union soldiers camped on the grounds, where a previous church then stood.

LaPlace

On the grounds of St. John the Baptist Parish offices, the Herbert Building, stands a cannon from the War.

Leesville

The Military Museum at Fort Polk, seven miles southeast of the Vernon Parish seat, includes War items.

At Burr Ferry Park (Louisiana highway 8, east bank of the Sabine River) west of town survive Confederate breastworks built late in the War to block an anticipated Union advance northward on the Sabine River.

LaSalle Parish

The LaSalle Museum Association, in the hamlet of Good Pine on U.S. 84, houses War weapons.

Mansfield State Commemorative Area

On the western edge of Louisiana occurred the South's last major victory of the War, when on April 8, 1864, fewer than 9,000

Confederate soldiers defeated 36,000 Union troops. A museum, monuments and library recall the encounter.

Battle of Pleasant Hill Park, in Sabine Parish not far south, commemorates another War encounter. At Keatchie, a village northwest of Mansfield, is a Confederate cemetery.

Marthaville

Rebel State Commemorative Area. The memorial area three miles northwest of town includes the site of an unknown Confederate soldier's grave. The soldier was killed April 1864 when wandering in the woods looking for his unit. The Barnhill family, local residents, buried the body and for nearly a century family members cared for the grave. As recently as 1962 a memorial was installed at the site, then designated a State Commemorative Area.

Napoleonville

Christ Episcopal Church. Leonidas Polk, the "fighting bishop of the Confederacy," dedicated the church, in which Union troops supposedly stabled their horses.

Natchitoches

Trinity Episcopal Church. In 1857 Polk laid the cornerstone of the church, construction of which was interrupted by the War.

Carroll House. The 1806 residence, also known as The Magnolia, served as the headquarters of Confederate general Richard Taylor, son of President Zachary Taylor.

Tante Hippe House. Slave quarters remain at the rear of the 1835 residence.

New Iberia

Shadows-on-the-Teche. The Union army made its headquarters in New Iberia during the 1864 Red River Campaign. Federal troops took control of the imposing 1834 "Shadows," centerpiece of an extensive sugar plantation established by planter David Weeks.

During the time Union forces occupied the manor house, Weeks's widow Mary, by then remarried, confined herself to the second floor where she died in 1863.

New Orleans

Confederate Museum. No less a figure than Jefferson Davis himself served on the planning committee for this museum, established in 1891. Although the former Confederate president died (1889) before the museum was completed, he returned post-mortem to the fanciful Romanesque-style structure two and a half years after his death when his body lay in state—after being disinterred from the Metairie Cemetery—prior to shipment to a cemetery in Richmond, Virginia. Exhibits at Memorial Hall, as the museum is called, include Davis family memorabilia, and such War items as uniforms, battle banners, photos, medical instruments, weapons, and paintings of Confederate generals. The book store-gift shop sells an interesting selection of items pertaining to the War.

P.G.T. Beauregard. Beauregard, a leading Southern general, served on the Confederate Museum's first board of directors. Various places in New Orleans recall his presence in the city. The 1826 Beauregard-Keyes House—named for him and for later resident novelist Francis Parkinson Keyes—was the general's residence for a time after the War. One room contains items which belonged to Beauregard and his family. In 1944 Keyes—whose book *Madame Castel's Lodger* tells of Beauregard's stay in the mansion—moved into the house. Beauregard (and his son) also lived after the War at 934 Royal Street, and he died on February 20, 1893, at 1631 Esplanade Avenue. An equestrian statue of Beauregard overlooks the Esplanade Avenue entrance to City Park. In June 1861 Beauregard sent part of a captured flagstaff from Fort Sumter—the general was in command when Confederates shelled the fort with the War's first shot—to New Orleans where the trophy was presented to the Orleans Guard at Gardette-Le Pretre House, 716 Dauphine. Before the War Beauregard served as engineer in charge when construction begun in 1848 at the Egyptian Revival-style Customs House, used by Union general Benjamin F. Butler when he occupied New Orleans. Locals nicknamed the reviled commander "Beast." It was "Beast" Butler who ordered carved on the base of the Jackson statue in Jackson Square the inscription, "The Union Must and Shall be Preserved."

Chalmette Battlefield. From 1880 to 1904 General Beauregard's son, Judge Réné Beauregard, occupied as a country residence the 1840 mansion at the Chalmette Battlefield, site of the 1815 Battle of New Orleans. The adjacent Chalmette National Cemetery was established in 1864 as a burial area for Union soldiers who died in Louisiana. A former powder magazine at the 1837 Jackson Barracks (occupied for a time by Confederate troops) a mile from the battlefield houses the Louisiana Military History and State Weapons Museum, with War items.

Museums. The Historic New Orleans Collection, housed in the restored 1792 Merieult House, includes items relating to the Federal occupation of the city during the War. Although New Orleans was occupied for fifteen years, starting in April 1862, plaques of the city's ruling governments in the bases of Canal Street light standards show New Orleans under "Confederate Domination, 1861-1865." In the colonnade of the Presbytere, part of the Louisiana State Museum, stands the *Pioneer*, launched by Confederates in the fall of 1861 as the world's first iron submarine. Built at a shipyard on Bayou St. John, the diminutive sub—six feet high and nineteen feet four inches long—required a crew of four. The ship, whose top speed was four miles per hour, never served in combat, completing only a trial run before Southerners sunk the vessel in Lake Ponchartrain to keep Federal troops from capturing the boat, later recovered as a relic of the War.

Monuments. At Lee Circle stands a bronze statue of Lee—looking north, as if on watch—perched atop a sixty foot shaft of Tennessee marble. Davis and Beauregard were present at the dedication in 1884. At 3400 Canal Street is a statue of Davis, who died in 1889 at the house of Judge Charles Fenner, 1134 First Street in the Garden District, after the Confederate leader, taken ill at Beauvoir, his house in Biloxi, Mississippi, was brought to New Orleans. Opposite the Davis statue is a monument to Charles Dreux, organizer of the Orleans Guards and the first New Orleans officer to die in the War. To the right of the entrance at Metairie Cemetery stands a statue of Confederate general Albert Sidney Johnston ("In His Honor, Impregnable; In His Simplicity, Divine," reads the inscription), killed at Shiloh on April 6, 1862. Beauregard and other Confederate soldiers are buried in the mausoleum beneath the statue. Atop a thirty-two foot granite shaft at the cemetery is a statue of "Stonewall" Jackson, while the mausoleum below contains the bodies of 2,500 men of the Army of Northern Virginia. A monument to Confederate dead at Greenwood Cemetery includes life-size busts of Jackson, Lee, Johnston and Leonidas Polk.

Hermann-Grima House. In 1850 Judge Felix Grima, whose family occupied the 1831 residence for five generations, bought the adjacent property for use as a stable, converted in 1881 to the Christian Woman's Exchange, established to raise money for impoverished widows of Confederate soldiers.

Nottoway

The huge house—supposedly the nation's largest plantation home—was spared during the War when a Union gunboat officer who had been a guest of sugar planter John Hampden Randolph, builder and owner of the mansion, decided not to shell it.

Opelousas

Governor's Mansion. When the Union occupied part of Louisiana Governor Henry W. Allen moved to Opelousas. Allen resided in the 1850 house of Homere Mouton, Louisiana's lieutenant governor in the late 1850s. Opposite the courthouse stood the LeCompte Hotel, Confederate capitol of Louisiana from May 1862 to January 1863.

Prudhomme House. The c. 1809 residence, the oldest structure in St. Landry Parish, was occupied by Union officers.

Jim Bowie Museum. The museum, installed in the tourist information center, includes War items.

Ray Homestead. The Confederate army used the house at the corner of Liberty and West Bellevue Streets as a medical facility. The owner of the property, Dr. George Hill, served as chief surgeon of the 2,000 man 9th Brigade Medical Department, headquartered at the house.

At Latwell, a village west of Opelousas, Matt's Museum includes a number of War related items.

Pineville

Mount Olivet Church. Union troops occupied the 1857 church as a barracks.

Alexandria National Cemetery. The burial ground, established in 1867, includes the graves of Confederate and Union troops.

Point Pleasant

In the cemetery lies General Paul O. Hebert, governor in the 1850s and the last commander of the Trans-Mississippi Department, which he surrendered after Lee's surrender at Appomattox.

Port Hudson State Commemorative Area

At a strategic point on the bluffs overlooking the Mississippi the Confederates established a fortification which served as the southern anchor of defenses along the river extending 150 miles north to Vicksburg. Reflecting Lincoln's observation that the Mississippi was the "key" to the Rebellion, the Union army targeted the Confederate strongholds at Vicksburg and Port Hudson. On May 23, 1863, some 30,000 Federal troops began a siege against 6,800 Rebels. On July 3 Lee's second invasion at Gettysburg was repelled, on July 4 Vicksburg fell, and on July 9—after a forty-eight day siege—Port Hudson finally succumbed, the last Confederate outpost on the Mississippi to surrender. Finally, the "key" was in the North's pocket. Six miles of trails, breastworks, a lookout tower at Fort Desperate, and a museum with interpretive displays recall the episode, a major factor in the Union's eventual victory.

St. Francisville

Locust Grove State Commemorative Area. This site, northeast of town, is a cemetery whose graves include that of Sarah Knox Taylor, Jefferson Davis's first wife. The burial ground is the only surviving part of Locust Grove Plantation, owned by the family of Davis's sister, Mrs. Anna E. Davis Smith. Davis brought his wife of three months (Zachary Taylor's daughter) to the plantation for a visit. Both contracted malaria, which proved fatal to Sarah, age twenty-one.

Grace Episcopal Church. In 1858 Leonidas Polk, the "fighting bishop of the Confederacy," laid the cornerstone of the church, severely damaged by shelling. Fighting was suspended for a day while Confederate and Union Masons attended a last rites service for their fellow Mason, John E. Hart, captain of the Federal gunboat U.S.S. *Albatross,* whose shells had rained down on the church just before his death. The rector of the church Hart's boat damaged officiated at his burial.

Cottage Plantation. The main house and ten original outbuildings, constructed between 1795 and 1850, survive as one of the few complete antebellum plantation properties, strongholds of the South's culture prior to the War.

Mount Carmel Church. Completed in 1893, the church was built from plans drafted in 1871 by P.G.T. Beauregard, a leading Southern general (see entry for Beauregard under New Orleans).

Printer's Cottage. The c. 1814 house, now a bed and breakfast establishment, includes the Civil War Room, its beams damaged by an 1863 gunboat attack on St. Francisville.

St. Joseph

Christ Church Rectory. The building, moved to the site in 1881, bears bullet holes and shrapnel scars from shelling by Union forces.

St. Maurice

The 1840 St. Maurice Plantation, outside town off U.S. 84, survived the War, as Union troops were forced to retreat to the west of the Red River, but the main house burned in 1981. The grounds, however, include a number of original structures. The two story galleried house which burned, called the Prothro Mansion, served as headquarters for General Zachary Taylor during the Mexican-American War. Among his officers who visited here were Grant, Lee and Davis.

Shreveport

Confederate Monument. The statue, dedicated in 1906, includes busts of Lee, "Stonewall" Jackson, Beauregard and Henry W. Allen. At the site, in June 1865, the Confederate flag was lowered for the last time in Louisiana.

Courthouse Square. In May 1863 the old courthouse became the Confederate capitol of Louisiana. The present structure dates from the 1920s.

Fort Humbug. This was one of three forts built when General Nathaniel Banks' campaign threatened this last Confederate stronghold in Louisiana during the spring 1864 Red River Campaign. A shortage of cannons forced the use of charred logs as "artillery" designed to humbug the Union attackers.

Oakland Cemetery includes graves of Confederate veterans.

Slidell

The name of the town and John Slidell Park commemorate the man appointed as a Confederate emissary to England during the War.

Sunset

South of town lies Chretien Point Plantation, a splendidly restored 1831 Greek Revival-style mansion house. During the Red River Campaign some of the skirmishes occurred on the plantation, which was looted and ravaged. A bullet hole in one of the front doors recalls the fighting. A stairway and window of the house were used as models for Tara, the plantation in the movie "Gone with the Wind."

On the banks of Bayou Bourbeau near Sunset a band of Confederate soldiers blocked a Union advance headed for Texas.

Tangipahoa

Camp Moore State Commemorative Area. The four acre site includes a cemetery with graves of several hundred Confederate soldiers. The museum contains War artifacts and exhibits on Camp Moore, one of the South's largest training camps. The base was named for Governor Thomas O. Moore, whose house Mooreland, near Alexandria, was burned by Union soldiers in 1864,

Thibodaux

St. John's Church. In the yard of the sanctuary, built in 1844 by Leonidas Polk, first bishop of Louisiana, stands a memorial to Polk, later a Southern general known as the "fighting bishop of the Confederacy." A slave gallery, now a choir loft, was added in 1856 to the building, supposedly the oldest Episcopal church west of the Mississippi.

Magnolia Plantation. The 1858 house, on Louisiana highway 311 south of town, served as a hospital during area encounters between Federal general Nathaniel Banks and Confederate general Richard Taylor.

Chatchie Plantation. On Louisiana highway 308 southwest of town stands an 1867 raised cottage built to replace an earlier house, called Homeplace, used as a field hospital during the Battle of

Lafourche Crossing. The battle site, marked by a plaque, can be seen from highways 308 and 1.

Washington

Nicholson House of History. The nineteenth century house, built by the first mayor of Washington, served as a Confederate hospital.

Winnfield

The Free State of Winnfield Historical Museum at the tourist center recalls the occasion when—after Louisiana seceded from the Union—Winn Parish seceded from Louisiana. Nonetheless, most area residents rallied to the Southern cause.

Salisbury Bridge, outside town, is at the site where in 1864 a Confederate unit blocked Federal forces sent to destroy the nearby Drake Salt Works. Some of the soldiers killed in the encounter repose in Old Harmony Cemetery. The salt deposit took its name from Reuben Drake, whose nephew Edwin Drake drilled the world's first oil well in Pennsylvania in 1841. The innovative rotary drill Drake used for the well had been tested by his uncle Reuben while drilling for water at the salt works.

Winter Quarters State Commemorative Area

Located south of Newellton, the long low-slung galleried house survived the War after Julia Nutt—whose Union sympathizing husband had fled to the North—crossed Federal lines to meet with Grant. She offered to feed and quarter Union troops if they refrained from destroying her home. Grant agreed, and although he burned all the other area plantation houses the Union general spared the Nutt house. The residence contains War weapons, uniforms, diaries and other items.

Kentucky

Augusta

In Augusta lived Senator Thornton F. Marshall, who cast the deciding vote which kept Kentucky in the Union. In May 1861 the state legislature decreed Kentucky's neutrality.

Joseph S. Tomlinson House. The house was built in 1823 as a residence for the president of Augusta College, the world's first Methodist college. Dr. Tomlinson was often visited here in the summer by his nephew, composer Stephen Foster, who wrote War era songs.

On September 27, 1862, a skirmish between Federal and Union troops in Augusta left twenty-one dead.

Barbourville

The first shot of the War in Kentucky was fired on Cumberland Avenue. On September 9, 1861, a skirmish took place at the Barbourville Bridge, north of town.

Bardstown

Civil War Museum. The museum at Old Bardstown Village, reproduction of a 1790 frontier community, includes a number of War artifacts.

The Mansion. The 1851 residence of William E. Johnson, Kentucky's first lieutenant governor and an acting governor, was the first place in the state to fly the Confederate flag, unfurled in 1861 before a crowd of some 5,000 onlookers. General John Hunt Morgan, known as the "Thunderbolt of the Confederacy" for his lightning-like raids, hid at The Mansion in 1863 after his escape from a Union prison. At the house lived Ben Johnson, a lawyer who defended members of Quantrill's Raiders, a Confederate guerrilla band. (See the Higginsville, Missouri entry.)

Old Talbott Tavern. The Lincoln family, including young Abe, stayed at the 1779 tavern during a trial involving a title dispute over the family farm. After losing the case, the Lincolns left the property and moved to Indiana.

Gertrude H. Smith House. Built in the early nineteenth century by the ominously named Colonel Ben Doom, the house served as a hospital during the War.

Edgewood. The 1819 columned mansion was headquarters of Confederate officer Braxton Bragg before the Battle of Perryville (see the entry for Perryville).

Spalding Hall. The building, constructed in 1819 and once the home of St. Joseph College, housed a hospital during the War. The Hall now contains the Bardstown Historical Museum, which includes War artifacts and displays. The Hall also houses the Oscar Getz Museum of Whiskey History, where one exhibit shows a copy of Lincoln's liquor license for the New Salem, Illinois, tavern he ran in the mid 1830s.

Miniature Soldier Museum. The museum contains more than 10,000 items, including toy figures recalling the War.

"My Old Kentucky Home." The house recalls composer Stephen Foster, whose songs evoke the old South, as it was before the War.

By the courthouse stands a slave auction stone (moved there from elsewhere) used for sales of blacks.

Bonnieville

Glen Lily. The house, which stood by the Green River, was the birthplace of Simon Bolivar Buckner, who both surrendered to Grant at Donelson (see the Tennessee entry for Fort Donelson National Battlefield) and served as a pallbearer at Grant's funeral.

Bowling Green

Riverview-Hobson House. Construction of the mansion was halted during the War so the Confederate army could use the structure as an ammunition depot. Atwood, Hobson's oldest son, became the youngest colonel in the Union army.

Western Kentucky University. The museum, which emphasizes Kentucky history, includes War items. The university lies on a hill occupied during the War by a fort. Campus walkways follow the lines of the old trenches.

Bowling Green was Kentucky's Confederate capital. Although the border state did not secede from the Union, the Confederacy admitted Kentucky as the South's thirteenth state.

Burnside

The General Burnside State Park was named for Union officer A.E. Burnside, whose headquarters were located in 1863 at Port Isabel, head of navigation on what was then the Cumberland River (now Lake Cumberland). The general's hair style—beard and moustache with clean-shaven chin—became known as a "burnsider"; the lateral hair patches eventually came to be called "sideburns."

Columbus

Columbus-Belmont State Park. The park occupies one of the most splendid vantage points—and militarily strategic points—on the entire Mississippi. Here, in early September 1861, 19,000 Confederate troops under General Leonidas Polk occupied the bluffs above the river, establishing there a fortress bristling with arms. Polk also stretched a chain across the Mississippi to block navigation of the waterway by Union vessels. Challenged by this attempt to occupy Kentucky, ostensibly neutral, and to control the Mississippi, Grant inaugurated his first active campaign of the War in November by attacking Belmont, a Confederate base in Missouri just across the river. Grant was forced to withdraw, but by February 1862 he managed to outflank Columbus, which he occupied the following month. In the park survive artillery, the anchor which was attached to the chain, and other relics of the Confederate stronghold. Artifacts and a video presentation at the museum recall the episode.

Covington

On Riverside Drive, in the northeast corner of Covington by the confluence of the Ohio and Licking Rivers, survive some restored War era houses. A statue on Kennedy Street depicts James Bradley, a black abolitionist active in the Underground Railroad.

Federal forces fortified the hills behind Covington to defend Cincinnati, just across the Ohio River. When Confederate troops approached the area in September 1862 Union soldiers crossed the river on a bridge formed by coal barges and blocked the advance near Fort Mitchell.

Cumberland Gap

See the entry in the Tennessee section.

Cynthiana

Battle Grove Cemetery. Confederate dead killed in the June 1864 Battle of Cynthiana repose in the graveyard, site of the June 12 encounter when John Hunt Morgan's raiders were overwhelmed by Union forces.

Danville

Centre College. Among the school's graduates was John C. Breckenridge, the youngest U.S. vice president and later a Confederate general.

Eddyville

Lyon County Museum. Exhibits include part of a telegraph used by Grant.

Elizabethtown

Ben Hardin Helm, a Confederate cavalry officer, lived in the town. Helm married Mary Todd Lincoln's sister, Emily. President Lincoln offered him the post of Union paymaster, a position Helm declined. He was killed on September 20, 1863, at Chickamauga in Georgia.

On the main square stands a building where an embedded cannonball remains as a souvenir of John Hunt Morgan's raid on Elizabethtown.

Fairview

A 351-foot-high Washington Monument-type tower—the nation's third highest obelisk—commemorates the place where Jefferson Davis was born on June 3, 1808. Near the 1929 monument, which offers wide-ranging panoramas from the observation area at the top, stands a reproduction of the two room log house where Davis was born. By an odd coincidence, Lincoln was also born in the same region at about the same time, so both Civil War presidents were born within one year and 100 miles of one another.

Flemingsburg

At a room in the Fleming Hotel James J. Andrews, War soldier of fortune, plotted the "Great Train Robbery," during which he captured the Confederate locomotive "The General." (See also the entry for Chattanooga, Tennessee.)

Frankfort

Frankfort was the only state capital which remained loyal to the Union to be captured by Confederate forces, who occupied the town from September 3 to October 4, 1862.

The Kentucky Military History Museum. The museum includes War related displays.

Kentucky First Ladies in Miniature. A series of dolls clad in period garb includes wives of the War era governors.

The Museum of the Kentucky Historical Society. The museum houses War documents, official papers and artifacts.

Some antebellum houses in Frankfort recall the War. The 1854 Carneal-Watson House served as headquarters for the Military

Board of Kentucky during the War. The c. 1820 Vest-Lindsey House was the boyhood home of George Graham Vest, Confederate Congressman and later a U.S. Senator for thirty-five years. The house was also occupied by Daniel Weisiger Lindsey, a Union general. Confederate general Fayette Hewitt lived at the 1817 Rodman-Hewitt House.

Georgetown

Georgetown College. At Giddings Hall—the first building erected at the oldest Baptist college west of the Alleghenies (1829)—a riot broke out in 1861 when Southern sympathizers tried to raise the Confederate flag.

Georgetown Cemetery. At the graveyard reposes George W. Johnson, first governor of Confederate Kentucky, mortally wounded at Shiloh.

Glasgow

At the Barren County courthouse grounds stand markers recalling the Christmas 1862 War skirmish, for which Southern participants were awarded the Confederate Medal of Honor.

Greensburg

In the old courthouse square is a marker commemorating the two Union generals from Greensburg, E.H. Hobson and W.T. Ward. The Union military governor, General Stephen G. Burbridge, ordered six Confederate prisoners shot here on November 19, 1864, for their killing of two Union soldiers.

Harrodsburg

Old Fort Harrod State Park. The park includes the cabin (moved from elsewhere) where Lincoln's parents married on June 2, 1806.

St. Philips Church. Confederate general Leonidas Polk conducted services at the Episcopal church before the Battle of Perry-ville.

Hawesville

At the 1822 Squire Pate House occurred Lincoln's first trial, in which he defended himself against charges of operating an Ohio River ferry without a license.

Hodgenville

Lincoln lore galore abounds in Hodgenville. A rather ponderous neo-classic granite building at the Abraham Lincoln Birthplace National Historic Site houses the supposed cabin in which the future War president was born. The fifty-six steps outside the granite building represent the number of years Lincoln lived.

Lincoln and his parents lived at nearby Knob Creek Farm for some six years (1811-1816). A reconstructed log cabin evokes the original residence.

The Lincoln Museum in Hodgenville contains twelve scenes from Lincoln's life, including such War era vignettes as the president drafting the Emancipation Proclamation, the Gettysburg Address, and the surrender at Appomattox. Exhibits and memorabilia upstairs at the museum also recall the man and the era.

Hopkinsville

Riverside Cemetery. Both Union and Confederate soldiers repose in the graveyard, where psychic Edgar Cayce is also buried.

Jackson

The Breathitt County Museum contains War artifacts.

Lebanon

The National Cemetery. Established in 1867, the burial ground contains War graves. When Colonel Tom Morgan's forces attacked Lebanon, located at the exact geographical center of Kentucky, on

July 5, 1863, Federal troops managed to delay his advance across the Ohio River.

Lexington

Mary Todd Lincoln House. Robert Todd—father of Mary Todd, Lincoln's wife—bought the c. 1806 residence in 1826. Mary lived there from age six to twenty-one when in 1839 she moved to Springfield, Illinois, to live with her sister. Some of her personal possessions are on display at the house.

Hunt-Morgan House. The c. 1814 Federal-style brick residence belonged to the famous Confederate general John Hunt Morgan. The Morgan Room contains displays of War memorabilia and exhibits on Morgan's Raiders, the unit led by the "Thunderbolt of the Confederacy," so called for his lightning-like raids. Morgan led his raiders farther north than any other unit in the Confederacy.

Bodley-Bullock House. The c. 1814 residence served as headquarters for both Union and Confederate forces.

Transylvania University. Old Morrison Hall (1833) on campus served as a prison and as a hospital for both sides during the War. John C. Breckinridge, born near Lexington and a law student at Translyvania, became the nation's youngest vice president (thirty-six), under James Buchanan, in 1857. He served as a general in the Confederate army and toward the end of the War became Secretary of State for the Confederacy. His statue stands in Cheapside Park. When Jefferson Davis attended Transylvania from 1821 to 1824 he roomed at the Ficklin House in Lexington. Other students at the school included Morgan and Albert Sidney Johnston, both Confederate generals.

Ashland. Three-time presidential candidate Henry Clay (1824, 1832, 1844) occupied the house from 1806 to his death in 1852. In his later years Clay, known as the "great compromiser," worked to preserve the Union.

Lexington Cemetery. The burial ground includes the graves of Clay, Morgan and members of Mary Todd's family.

Louisville

The Filson Club. The historical society, established in 1884, houses manuscripts and other items pertaining to the War.

Jefferson County Courthouse. The state legislature assembled here when Confederate forces occupied Frankfort in September 1862.

The Confederate monument at South Third and Shipp Streets belies the fact that Louisville remained a Union city, serving the north as a major supply base and medical center.

Maysville

Rand-Richeson Academy. The old boys school numbers among its graduates Grant, who lived in town for a time with his uncle, Peter Grant, now buried in the graveyard behind the library.

Mill Creek

The cemetery includes graves of Lincoln's relatives, among them Bersheba Lincoln, his grandmother, and Mary Lincoln (Crume) and Nancy Lincoln, his aunts.

Mill Springs

Located on the southeast side of Lake Cumberland, the mill here—which boasts one of the world's largest overshot water wheels—offers an audiovisual program on the area's War history. General Felix Zollicoffer and more than 100 other Confederate dead, killed in a January 19, 1862 battle, are buried in a mass grave at a cemetery near Nancy.

Morganfield

Bethal Baptist Church. Former slave Elisha W. Green founded the church, destroyed by fire in 1977, in 1845.

On the courthouse lawn Lincoln delivered the only political speech he gave in his native state.

The Union County Museum includes War items.

Morgantown

Butler County Courthouse. On the grounds stands a monument to both Confederate and Union soldiers, a rare example of a dual memorial honoring both sides.

Munfordville

Francis Asbury Smith House. Confederate general Braxton Bragg occupied the c. 1835 house as a headquarters. Bragg's forces used the 1830s Presbyterian church as a hospital. Across the street stands a one story house—originally two separate brick structures connected by a passageway—where nurses who worked at the hospital lived. A marker in town recalls the September 1862 Battle of Munfordville.

Newport

Taylor Mansion. The 1837 house formed a link in the Underground Railroad. Escaped slaves headed north hid in the basement.

Nicholasville

Some 3,000 Union soldiers repose at the Camp Nelson Cemetery. At Camp Dick Robinson, south of town, operated the first Union recruiting station south of the Ohio River.

Owensboro

At the former Riley Plantation on U.S. 60 (designated in this area the Josiah Henson Trail) stood the cabin of slave Josiah Henson, thought by some to have inspired Harriet Beecher Stowe's 1852 anti-slavery novel *Uncle Tom's Cabin.* In Owensboro during the summer of 1993 was held the premier of *Josiah!*, a musical based on Henson's life. (See the entry for Chopin, Louisiana, which also claims Uncle Tom as a local character.)

Paducah

Lloyd Tilghman House. The railroad builder and Confederate general occupied the house from 1852 to 1861. A statue on Fountain Avenue in Lang Park honors the West Point graduate, killed at the Battle of Vicksburg after being struck by a cannonball.

First Baptist Church. The original 1840 building served as a hospital for Union soldiers.

Market House. The 1850 second Market House, which preceded the present 1905 building, was used as a hospital when Federal troops occupied the area.

In response to the early September 1861 Confederate occupation of Columbus and Hickman, Kentucky towns on the Mississippi River not far west of Paducah, on September 6 Grant led 5,000 men into Paducah where they marched down Broadway to the levee on the Ohio river. Grant issued a proclamation to the citizens of Paducah, noting that the "strong arm of the government is here to protect its friends and punish its enemies." So began the Civil War in the west.

Perryville

Perryville Battlefield State Historic Site. Here occurred the most important of the 400 military encounters in Kentucky. Nearly 40,000 troops clashed on October 8, 1862, in what one Union general described as "the bloodiest battle of modern times." More than 7,500 casualties occurred during the battle, an episode in the Confederate attempt to gain control of central Kentucky. After securing the Union supply base in Louisville, General Don Carlos Buell advanced to engage the Southerners at Perryville. Following the encounter, Buell allowed the Confederates to retreat unhindered, a concession which led to his removal as Union commander. A museum contains artifacts, displays and a diorama of the battle.

The mansion now housing Elmwood Inn at Perryville, an attractive restaurant known for its bourbon-laced sauces, served after the battle as a hospital.

Pike County

In this county at the far eastern edge of Kentucky lived the McCoy clan, which engaged in a long feud with the Hatfield family of Mingo County in adjacent West Virginia. The feud originated during the War when Anderson "Devil Anse" Hatfield, leader of a guerrilla band during the conflict, was accused of killing Harmon McCoy, a Union sympathizer, on February 1, 1863. The dispute over this matter touched off the feud between the families, which supported opposing sides during the War. The mini Civil War between the Hatfields and the McCoys lasted for some thirty years, during which nearly forty members of the families were killed.

Pikeville. A marker in the city park indicates where future president James A. Garfield took the oath as a Union brigadier general in January 1862.

Richmond

Harris House. The 1813 residence was named for Dr. John McCord Harris, who treated wounded soldiers in the house after the August 29-30, 1862, Battle of Richmond.

Courthouse. The ornamental iron fence which once surrounded the grounds of the 1850 courthouse served to hold Union prisoners. Part of the fence is now at Richmond Cemetery, where Cassius M. Clay (see entry for White Hall) is buried.

Solomon Smith House. Union troops captured in August 1862 by General E. Kirby Smith's forces were paroled at the house.

McCreary House. The War officer and later U.S. Senator and two-time governor of Kentucky lived at the house.

The tourist office in Richmond offers a brochure and tape for a War battles driving tour from Richmond to Berea.

Russellville

A marker downtown recalls that the town served as the first capital of Kentucky after the Confederacy admitted the state in December 1861. Delegates from around the state met in

Russellville on November 18 to form a provisional Confederate government.

Bibb House. At the c. 1822 house lived Mayor Richard Bibb, a Revolutionary War veteran and early-day Abolitionist.

Springfield

The 1816 Washington County courthouse contains the 1806 marriage documents of Thomas Lincoln and Nancy Hanks, parents of the future president.

Lincoln Homestead State Park. Located five miles north of town, the park includes a replica of the 1782 cabin which belonged to Lincoln's father and the original cabin of his mother.

Vanceburg

The 1884 Union soldier statue on the courthouse lawn is claimed to be the only non-funerary monument south of the Ohio River to Federal troops killed in the War.

Versailles

The Versailles Historical Park memorializes eight War generals and also a Kentucky governor.

Washington

In the summer of 1833 Harriet Beecher (Stowe), while visiting her pupil Elizabeth Key, witnessed a slave auction at the block in front of the courthouse, a scene she evoked in *Uncle Tom's Cabin,* a novel which agitated anti-slavery sentiment and contributed to the mood which led to the War. Elizabeth, one of the six children of Colonel and Mrs. Marshall Key, lived with her family in the still existing 1807 house on Main Street.

Also on Main Street stands the c. 1800 house (now the visitor center) of lawyer and Abolitionist James A. Paxton, who hid runaway slaves under the stairwell at the adjacent Paxton Inn until they could continue north by the Underground Railroad.

In a c. 1797 house was born in 1803 Albert Sidney Johnston, Commander of the Confederate Army of the West and believed to be the highest ranking officer killed in action during the War. He died at Shiloh on April 6, 1862.

Water Valley

Camp Beauregard, the only Confederate training camp in Kentucky, was located east of the village.

White Hall

This estate—located in central Kentucky southeast of Louisville and south of Lexington—belonged to Cassius Clay, an outspoken opponent of slavery who became a national figure in the Abolitionist movement, published an Abolitionist newspaper, and served as a major general in the Union army. The colorful Clay fought his opponents not only with words but, on occasion, also with pistols, his hickory cane and a Bowie knife. The forty-four room three story brick c. 1799 mansion contains War era furnishings.

Wickliffe

Just south of town stood Fort Jefferson where—after Confederate forces seized nearby Columbus in September 1861—Union troops established a supply base on the Mississippi to serve the Western Theater.

Zollicoffer Park and Logan's Crossroads Cemetery

A 1911 monument at the site, nine miles west of Somerset, marks the January 1862 battle during which Confederate general Felix Zollicoffer was killed.

Tennessee

Ashland City

North of town, on Sycamore Creek, stood the 1835 Sycamore Powder Mill, which produced a huge amount of gunpowder for the Confederacy. At one time the DuPont Company operated the mill.

Beersheba Springs

When General Braxton Bragg withdrew from the area to fortify Chattanooga, the town was left outside Confederate lines and remained undefended. Marauders—some of them deserters from both sides—looted the hotel, now the United Methodist Assembly meeting area.

Bolivar

Union generals Grant, Sherman, Logan and McPherson occupied Magnolia Manor, now a bed and breakfast, as a headquarters.

Brentwood

At Windy Hill, an 1820s country house southeast of town, the owner hid valuables as well as horses and cows in the basement to protect them from Federal marauders during the War. (See also the entry for Franklin.)

Brownsville

College Hill Center houses a collection of books and memorabilia relating to Lincoln.

The Confederate monument at the courthouse honors not only the War dead but also the women of Haywood County.

Chattanooga

The Chickamauga and Chattanooga National Military Park,

mainly in Georgia south of Chattanooga, recalls a series of pivotal autumn 1863 encounters. The Battle of Chickamauga in September, one of the War's bloodiest encounters, resulted in nearly 4,000 dead and another 30,000 wounded and missing. The South's failure to pursue the defeated Yankee forces enabled them to regroup under Grant and defeat the Confederates at the Battles of Lookout Mountain and Missionary Ridge on November 23-25. The victory opened the so- called Gateway to the West, enabling Sherman to begin his devastating "March to the Sea" through Georgia.

Point Park (accessible only to pedestrians) at the north edge of Lookout Mountain, and Bragg's Reservation and Sherman's Reservation on Missionary Ridge at the eastern side of town, comprise areas where the encounters unfolded. Many of the private homes on Crest Drive on the top of Missionary Ridge display in their yards cannons and historical markers. The Ochs Museum and the Cravens House on Lookout contain War era displays. The Confederama at the bottom of Lookout offers a 480 square foot reproduction of the battle terrain, with an electronically controlled depiction of the fighting.

The 1863 National Cemetery and the 1865 Confederate Cemetery contain the graves of fallen troops. Buried at the National Cemetery are James J. Andrews and seven of his men, their graves marked by a replica of "The General," the Confederate steam locomotive they seized near Marietta, Georgia, in April 1862.

The six mile long steam train excursion from the Tennessee Valley Railroad Museum passes over a bridge and through a tunnel connected with the Battle of Chattanooga.

The Chattanooga Regional History Museum contains War exhibits.

The *Daily Rebel* began publication, at 523 Market Street, on August 2, 1862. At one time the newspaper was forced to publish in boxcars traveling with Confederate troops. The last issue appeared at Selma, Alabama, on April 11, 1865.

Clarksville

Greenwood Cemetery. A Confederate Monument—a soldier statue atop a column flanked below by other figures—honors War dead.

Emerald Hill. Gustavus A. Henry, Confederate senator and well known political orator, lived at the 1830s house.

The old Kennedy and Glenn's Bank, which stood on the west side of the town square, smuggled funds and securities to England for safekeeping during the War.

At nearby Fort Defiance by the Cumberland River survive well preserved earthen breastworks.

The Visitor Center and Museum at Fort Campbell, north of town, include a few War relics.

Columbia

Advance and Retreat. At this country house three miles south of town Army of Tennessee commander John Bell Hood established his headquarters on November 24, 1864. A month later an order for the Army's retreat was issued from the house.

At Chapel Hill, east of Columbia, a monument indicates the site of the cabin where Nathan Bedford Forrest, the pesky Confederate general, was born on July 13, 1821.

Cumberland Gap National Historical Park

The Pinnacle, the high point in the park, was the site of War trenches. To defend the Gap, which changed hands several times during the War, the Confederates emplaced "Long Tom," then the largest kind of gun in use, in the lowlands. Three months after Federal troops captured the Gap on June 17, 1862, they were forced to retreat, only to recapture the strategic pass on September 9, 1863.

Elizabethton

Andrew Johnson, Lincoln's successor (see the entry for

Greeneville), died in 1875 at the home of his daughter, Mary Johnson Stover, located north of the Watauga River outside town.

Nathan Bedford Forrest State Historic Area

The site commemorates the place where in November 1864 the Confederate general's forces secured a commanding artillery vantage point over the Tennessee River at Pilot Knob. From the height the Southerners shelled a Federal supply and munitions depot below, and also fired on a supply convoy. This attack resulted in the first defeat in history of a naval force by a cavalry unit.

Fort Donelson National Battlefield

At Fort Donelson the Union, its forces led by Grant, won its first major victory of the War. The loss of the fort after a four day battle in February 1862 proved devastating to the Confederate cause. With the victory the North gained control of the Cumberland and Tennessee Rivers, thus breaking the Southern defense line from the Alleghenies to the Mississippi. This opened the way for the invasion of the South.

Sights at the park include a Confederate Monument, a National Cemetery with 655 Union dead, the Dover Hotel where General Simon B. Buckner surrendered the fort and 13,000 men to Grant, and the riverside battery which on February 14 saw an exchange of "iron valentines."

When Buckner asked his opponent the surrender terms, Grant replied, "No terms except an unconditional and immediate surrender can be accepted." With the capture of Fort Donelson and, on February 6, the nearby Fort Henry on the Tennessee River fifteen miles to the west, the Union won key victories and found a new hero—U.S. ("Unconditional Surrender") Grant. The six and a half mile Fort Henry Road at Land Between the Lakes passes a turnoff to hiking trails which follow the retreat route of Southern forces from Fort Henry to Fort Donelson.

Fort Pillow State Historical Area

Original breastworks and a reconstructed fort recall the outpost, built to help the South control the Mississippi River. In the early summer of 1862 shelling by Federal gunboats forced the evacuation of the fort by the Confederates, who recaptured it in April 1864 with an attack led by Nathan Bedford Forrest.

Franklin

In and around the picturesque town swirled War clashes. For four years Federal troops who occupied the area were garrisoned at 1863 Fort Granger—where traces of trenches, gun replacements and walls remain—overlooking the town. On November 30, 1864, Confederate general John Bell Hood attacked General John Schofield's Federal forces in the Battle of Franklin. The North lost 2,000 men, the South three times as many, including five generals taken to Carnton, a nearby 1826 country estate. They were buried elsewhere, but at Carnton repose nearly 1,500 soldiers at the nation's only privately owned and maintained War cemetery.

Carter House. Bullet holes in the walls recall that the residence changed hands several times during the battle. Displays at the house include War artifacts.

St. Paul's. The state's oldest Episcopal church (1834) served as a hospital. Soldiers took its furnishings to use as firewood.

Gant House. Sally Ewin Gant used a trap door in the roof of the house to spy on Union activities.

Between Franklin and Brentwood to the north lie Creekside, whose still bloodstained floors recall that the house was used as a hospital after the Battle of Franklin; Green Pastures, where Forrest and his men camped before the Battle of Nashville; and Mooreland, used by both sides as a hospital. At Century Oaks, northeast of Franklin, the owners supposedly blindfolded their horses and led them up a circular staircase to the third floor ballroom to hide the animals from Federal raiders.

Gatlinburg

Near the town was born on October 18, 1818, John H. Reagan, Postmaster General and Acting Treasury Secretary of the Confederacy.

Greeneville

Courthouse. The yard is one of the few places with monuments honoring both Confederate and Union soldiers. This recalls how the region suffered from divided loyalties. Union sympathizers met in Greeneville in 1861 in an attempt to make East Tennessee a separate state. One marker memorializes General John Hunt Morgan, "The Thunderbolt of the Confederacy," killed September 4, 1864, after a Union sympathizer revealed his whereabouts.

Cumberland Presbyterian Church. A cannonball from a War shelling remains embedded in the wall of the sanctuary.

Andrew Johnson. Lincoln's successor, North Carolina native Andrew Johnson, came to Greeneville in the 1820s at age seventeen and began his political career there. Johnson's tailor shop and his solid looking brick house—the family home from 1851 to 1875—recall the seventeenth president's time in Greeneville. Johnson and members of his family are buried in the Andrew Johnson National Cemetery where an urn-decorated monument topped by an eagle marks his grave.

Harrogate

Lincoln Memorial University. The Lincoln Museum on the campus of the school contains an extensive collection of materials relating to the president and the War. The holdings include not only displays but also books, manuscripts, photos, paintings and artifacts. Lincoln's friend, General O.O. Howard, established the university in 1897 in the area designated by the president during an 1863 meeting between the two men.

Hendersonville

Monthaven Bed and Breakfast House was used as a hospital during the War.

Henning

The childhood home (1921-1929) of Alex Haley, author of *Roots*, Henning developed after the War. But Bethlehem Methodist church (1830), established a mile east of the present town, housed wounded brought to the sanctuary after the battle at Fort Pillow, on the Mississippi to the west. Those who died were buried in the 1840 Bethlehem Cemetery, which now includes the Haley family plot. Haley himself is buried in the yard of his childhood house.

Jackson

James S. Lyons House. During the weeks preceding the April 1862 Battle of Shiloh, Grant occupied the residence, which stood at 512 East Main Street, as a headquarters.

Riverside Cemetery includes graves of unknown Confederate soldiers.

Near Britton's Lane, south of town, a monument to soldiers killed in a September 1, 1862, encounter honors the combatants, some buried here.

Johnson City

A monument at Lamont and Tennessee Streets marks the site of the 1861 Confederate training camp.

Knoxville

Confederate Memorial Hall. The antebellum mansion, also known as "Bleak House" (for the popular Charles Dickens novel of the time), was used by Confederate general James Longstreet as his headquarters during the November 1863 siege of Knoxville. The house contains war era artifacts and furniture.

Speedwell Manor. Built c. 1830 by slave labor in Tazewell,

Tennessee, the house—moved to its present location—includes a window sill with an inscription written by a Confederate soldier as he watched the burning of Tazewell.

Volunteer State Veterans Hall of Honor. The shrine includes both Union and Confederate artifacts, a reminder of the divided loyalties in East Tennessee.

Three burial grounds in Knoxville—Confederate, National and Old Gray Cemeteries—contain War graves.

Various markers around Knoxville indicate points of interest relating to the November 1863 siege when Confederate troops tried unsuccessfully to recapture the city they had evacuated in August. Fort Byington, which stood near the main entrance to the University of Tennessee and Fort Sanders on the campus, along with Forts Dickerson and Stanley near present day Chapman Highway south of the Tennessee River, served as the Union's main defensive points. Confederate forces camped during the siege at the site of Knoxville College, while Union general Ambrose Burnside occupied as his headquarters the J.H. Crozier House, on the site of the old Farragut Hotel, now the First Tennessee Bank Building.

LaGrange

This unspoiled nineteenth century hamlet fifty miles east of Memphis includes such time haunted houses as 1834 Twin Gables, occupied by various Union officers; 1850 Hancock Hall, used by Grant as a headquarters in 1862; Woodlawn, a hospital and a headquarters for Sherman; and Westover of Woodstock, where Lucy Holcombe (Pickens) grew up. Known as the "Queen of the Confederacy," she was the only woman whose portrait appeared on the Confederacy currency. Holcombe became the third wife of Francis Wilkinson Pickens, U.S. Congressman from 1834 to 1843 and governor of South Carolina, which seceded on December 18, 1860, two days after he took office.

Immanuel Episcopal Church. The pews of the 1832 church

were made into coffins for Union dead. The church served as a hospital and barracks.

Lebanon

Cedar Grove Cemetery. The 1899 Confederate monument bears an unusual inscription enumerating the number of soldiers, fatalities, prisoners and the public debt involved with the War.

Memphis

Confederate Park. The park, which overlooks the Mississippi, offered a vantage point for Memphis citizens who watched as Union gunboats sank six of the seven defending Southern vessels on June 6, 1862. After a brief (ninety minutes) encounter the Northerners demanded the surrender of Memphis, to which Mayor John Park responded, "The city is in your hands." On the south side of the park is a plaque summarizing the Confederate history of Memphis. Facing Front Street stands a statue of Jefferson Davis who worked in Memphis in the insurance business after the War. A plaque at 129 Court Avenue marks the site where Davis lived from 1867 to 1875. The original Confederate cannons which stood in the park were taken in 1942 in a scrap metal drive during a later war.

Malmo Building. The 1842 office building, the city's oldest commercial structure, was used during the War as a hospital for Union troops awaiting passage north on Mississippi River boats.

Gayoso Hotel. At the 1842 hotel, which stood on Front Street, William Forrest, brother of General Nathan Bedford Forrest, supposedly rode his horse into the lobby on August 21, 1864, looking for Union commander Stephen A. Hurlbut. The general died on October 27, 1877, in the Memphis home of another brother, Colonel Jesse Forrest, who lived at 693 Union Avenue. An equestrian statue in Forrest Park marks the grave of Nathan and his wife Mary.

Elmwood Cemetery. Confederate soldiers, along with many

Memphis notables, repose in the city's most historical burial ground.

Leonidas Polk and, later, Grant occupied the house which stood at 533 Beale Street.

From the old Union Planters Bank building on Madison the press and type of the *Memphis Daily Appeal* were removed on June 6, 1862—the day before the city was occupied—for shipment to Grenada and later Jackson, Mississippi, eventually going to Columbus, Georgia, as the paper continued to publish until Union troops finally destroyed the equipment and scattered the type. Called a "moving *Appeal*" by Sherman's troops, the paper resumed publication in Memphis on November 5, 1865.

Murfreesboro

Stones River National Battlefield. The 350 acre park recalls the three day battle, which started December 31, 1862, involving more than 80,000 soldiers and resulting in 23,000 casualties. A self-guided driving tour includes what is supposedly the nation's earliest War monument, the boxy looking stone block 1863 Hazen Brigade Monument. An audio-visual presentation at the museum explains the battle. The National Cemetery contains the graves of 6,100 Union soldiers.

Courthouse. The 1859 Rutherford County Courthouse and the Federal garrison in town were targets of a July 1862 dawn raid by Confederate cavalry under Forrest.

Fortress Rosecrans. Located west of town at Stones River, this was the largest earthworks fort built by the Union during the War. The installation originally covered 200 acres and included a huge supply base which provisioned troops for the attack on Chattanooga. Some of the earthworks, which averaged fifteen feet high, remain.

In a house which stood on East Main Street, General Leonidas Polk, the "Fighting Bishop of the Confederacy," officiated at the December 14, 1862, marriage of John Hunt Morgan, the "Thunderbolt of the Confederacy." Groomsmen included Generals Braxton Bragg and John C. Breckinridge, former U.S. vice president.

Evergreen Cemetery. Unknown Confederate soldiers killed in the Battle of Murfreesboro are buried here.

Nashville

Capitol. At the state capitol stands a statue of Sam Davis, executed in November 1863 as a Confederate spy (see the entry for Smyrna).

Tennessee State Museum. The museum opened a new wing in the early 1980s to display War materials. Photos, drawings and artifacts recall the War in Tennessee.

Belle Meade. The elegant mansion—once the centerpiece of a 5,300 acre plantation and horse farm—served as headquarters for Confederate general James R. Chalmers during the December 15-16, 1864, Battle of Nashville, the last major encounter in the state.

Travellers' Rest. At the 1779 house, residence of John Overton, a friend and political advisor to Andrew Jackson, Confederate general John B. Hood made his headquarters. A key encounter during the Battle of Nashville—the Battle of Peach Orchard Hill—occurred on the grounds of the property.

Vanderbilt. On campus survive breastworks which formed part of the seven mile long defensive lines that ran southwest across the city. At Shy's Hill, where the Confederates made one of their last stands, the earthworks are still visible.

Opposite the entrance to The Hermitage, Jackson's house, lies the Confederate Cemetery. Most of the 483 soldiers buried here died at the Confederates Soldiers' Home, which stood about one mile to the north.

Downtown Presbyterian Church. Union soldiers used the church as a hospital.

At a house at 511 5th Avenue South lived Captain William Driver, a mariner who in 1831 dubbed an American flag he received as a present "Old Glory"; by 1850 the name had become common for the flag in general. When he lived in Nashville during the War, Driver concealed the flag by making it into a quilt. Union troops flew the flag at the capitol when they took the city.

Puluski

Sam Davis Museum. The museum, which houses War memorabilia, occupies the site where the "Boy Hero of the Confederacy" was executed as a spy on November 27, 1862 (see the entry for Smyrna). In courthouse square stands a monument to Davis. A plaque on the old law office of Judge Thomas Jones notes that the Ku Klux Klan was founded in Pulaski on December 24, 1865.

Rogersville

Hale Springs Inn. On the town square stands the state's oldest hostelry in continuous operation—since 1824, except during the War when Union soldiers used the inn as a headquarters.

Savannah

Cherry Mansion. The house, in the western outskirts of town, was used as a headquarters by Union commander C.F. Smith, who died here. His successor was Major General Ulysses S. Grant, who breakfasted at the house just as gunfire broke out at Pittsburg Landing—prelude to the imminent encounter at Shiloh.

Sewanee

At the secluded college town repose Southern officers Kirby Smith and Jack Eggleston, the last full Confederate general and last naval officer, both of whom died at Sewanee. In October 1860 at the University of the South, Leonidas Polk laid the main building's cornerstone, which Union soldiers later broke into pieces as souvenirs.

Shiloh National Military Park

More military encounters (over 800) took place in Tennessee—the last state to secede and the first to be readmitted to the Union after the War—than in any state other than Virginia. Shiloh is one of the state's four War related National Military Parks.

After Confederate general Albert S. Johnston attacked Grant's forces encamped on the Tennessee River on April 6, 1862, the Northerners counterattacked the following day and forced the Southern army to retreat to Corinth, Mississippi. Johnston, who Jefferson Davis considered the finest officer in the War, bled to death after a rifle ball severed an artery in his leg. Monuments, graves (the National Cemetery overlooks Pittsburg Landing and the Tennessee River) and a museum recall the famous battle. During the fighting about one-quarter of the 100,000 combatants were killed, wounded or captured—more casualties than of the Revolutionary War, War of 1812 and Mexican-American War combined. The encounter at Shiloh shattered the illusions of both sides that victory would be easy. After Shiloh, Grant said, "I gave up all ideas of saving the Union, except by complete conquest."

Smyrna

Sam Davis Home. The 1810 house commemorates the twenty-one year old Confederate soldier captured behind Union lines on November 19, 1863, while carrying secret papers to General Braxton Bragg, then near Chattanooga. Federal authorities tried Davis as a spy and sentenced him to death. Davis rode to the gallows in Pulaski (see the entry for that city) on November 27 perched atop the coffin used to bury him.

Tiptonville

A marker at the Lake County courthouse recalls the battle for Island Number 10 in the Mississippi and the capture of Tiptonville by Union Forces in April 1862.

Tullahoma

The Army of Tennessee made its headquarters in Tullahoma during the first half of 1863. At a Confederate cemetery repose more than 400 Southern soldiers.

Union City

Dixie Gun Works. On display is a firearms collection with some 1,500 antique revolvers and rifles, many dating from the nineteenth century and earlier.

The Confederate Cemetery includes graves of soldiers killed during Forrest's December 23, 1862, raid. A Confederate monument in the town square bears an unusual inscription, memorializing Southern soldiers "killed in battle...[or] starved in Federal prison" who preserved the South's "Anglo-Saxon civilization."

Winchester

Citizens meeting at the Franklin County courthouse voted on February 24, 1861, to secede from Tennessee. The group petitioned the state of Alabama to annex the country. This attempt to join the Confederacy became unnecessary after Tennessee seceded on June 24.

Arkansas

Arkansas Post

Arkansas Post National Memorial. In 1686 French explorers carved an outpost out of the wilderness and established near the confluence of the Mississippi and the Arkansas Rivers the first European settlement in the lower Mississippi valley. The frontier town prospered, then declined when the state capital was moved to Little Rock in 1821. The area enjoyed—or suffered from—one last moment of gory glory when 5,000 Confederate soldiers defended Fort Hindman, built near the old town on the banks of the

Arkansas, during a January 10 and 11, 1863, attack by Federal gunboats and 30,000 Union soldiers under General John A. McClernand. The bombardment severely damaged the fort and destroyed many of the old buildings of the Arkansas Post settlement, which eventually disappeared. A visitor center with history displays and walkways through the site recall the early day town.

Arkansas Post County Museum. The museum (located on the main highway outside the National Memorial) includes War items, such as a copy of the July 2, 1863 *Vicksburg Daily Citizen* printed on wallpaper due to the lack of newsprint.

Benton

Shoppach House. Both sides occupied the small 1853 brick residence, which now houses antiques and history displays.

Berryville

Saunders Memorial Museum. The extensive gun collection includes War era weapons, among them firearms belonging to Jesse James, desperado and guerrilla of the time.

Cabot

Camp Nelson Confederate Cemetery. At the burial ground repose some 500 Southern soldiers from Texas and Arkansas who died during a measles epidemic while stationed at a nearby base. A rough-hewn stone monument, installed in 1905, commemorates the unknown deceased.

Camden

McCollum-Chidester House. Confederate general Sterling Price and Union general Frederick Steele both, in turn, occupied the eleven room 1847 house as a headquarters at the time of the Battle of Poison Spring (see the entry for Poison Spring). Bullet holes in upstairs walls supposedly originated during a Confederate attack. The house contains original furniture of the era used when the Chidester family lived there.

Confederate Cemetery. Seven rows of gravestones around a tall marble shaft indicate the last resting place of more than 200 Confederate soldiers, some of them killed at Poison Spring and Jenkins' Ferry (see those entries).

Fort Lookout. Confederate general Edmund Kirby Smith built earthen fortifications to defend Camden. Rifle trenches and cannon pits remain on the bluff overlooking the Ouachita River.

Cypress Bend

Henry M. Stanley. The hamlet of Cypress Bend, once located on the Arkansas River a few miles upstream from Arkansas Post, disappeared in the 1860s when flood waters washed the settlement away. At Cypress Bend lived Henry M. Stanley, who as a boy worked as a storekeeper for his foster father, Louis Altshul, until the War began. Stanley then joined the Arkansas Volunteers, and was later captured at Shiloh. After his release, Stanley enlisted in the Union army, then later served in the Union navy. After the War Stanley became famous as the journalist who located explorer David Livingston in Africa.

Dardanelle

Dardanelle Rock. From atop the sheer rocky formation overlooking the Arkansas River Confederate soldiers spied on Federal activities in the area.

Doddridge

After the Emancipation Proclamation, former slaves homesteaded the East Kiblah community at Doddridge, located in the far southwestern corner of Arkansas. During the War, when the community was known as "The Bend," Union and Confederate soldiers took refuge there. The former Kiblah school now serves as a community center.

Fayetteville

Headquarters House. Both sides at various times occupied the restored residence, built in 1853 by Judge Jonas Tebbetts, a strong Union supporter. The Union command used the house as a headquarters during the April 1863 Battle of Fayetteville.

Walker Stone House. Judge David Walker, chairman of the Arkansas Secession Convention, lived in the house. The "Stone" refers not to the structure's building material, which is brick, but to a later occupant—Edward Durrell Stone, the world famous architect.

Confederate Cemetery. At the burial ground, located by the base of Mt. Sequoyah, repose Southern soldiers from Arkansas, Missouri, Texas and Louisiana.

Fort Smith

National Cemetery. The nation's oldest national cemetery—established in 1818 as part of the original military post—includes War graves, among them that of Confederate general James B. McIntosh. Some 1,600 Union soldiers repose at the cemetery.

Old Fort Museum. Displays of the area's military history between 1817 and 1970 include War relics.

Sebastian County Courthouse. On the grounds stands a Confederate monument, installed here rather than at the national cemetery as Federal officials objected that the monument's inscription failed to include a reference to Union soldiers buried at the cemetery.

Harrison

Boone County Heritage Museum. Displays at the museum include War medical instruments.

Robinson Museum. The museum, on highway 65 southeast of Harrison, includes War items.

Helena

War Markers. Markers around town recall episodes in the July 4, 1863, Battle of Helena.

Fort Curtis. One marker on Perry Street indicates the site of Fort Curtis, erected in August 1862 by Union forces as the centerpiece of the city's five fortified Federal positions. With the help of the gunboat *Tyler,* the 4,129-strong Union forces successfully defended against 7,646 Confederate attackers, who hoped to occupy Helena and then relieve the Federal siege at Vicksburg. The same day that the Battle of Helena occurred proved disastrous for the South elsewhere; on July 4, Vicksburg fell to Grant and Lee withdrew in defeat at Gettysburg.

Granny Holmes. Confederate soldiers at Helena nicknamed their aged commander, Theophilus Holmes, "Granny" as the feeble old man scarcely presented a commanding appearance. While defending Arkansas Post to the south the previous January, "Granny" ordered his forces to "hold the place until every man is dead," a do-or-die attitude received rather unenthusiastically in the ranks.

Confederate Cemetery. On a steep hillside tucked away at the back of Maple Hill Cemetery nestles a small Confederate graveyard, with moss-bearded markers in a shadowed grove. A pillar topped by a soldier statue memorializes unknown Confederate dead. Helena was the home of seven Southern generals, several of them buried at the cemetery.

Phillips County Museum. The collection includes War artifacts.

Jacksonport State Park

In the late eighteenth century the town of Jacksonport developed near the confluence of the Black and White Rivers. The settlement began as a trading center, and later became a steamboat port and the county seat. Thanks—or no thanks—to its strategic location by the rivers, the town was occupied by both armies, with five generals using Jacksonport as a headquarters at various times. On June 5, 1865, General Jeff Thompson, called the "Swamp Fox of the Confederacy," surrendered 6,000 troops to Union lieutenant colonel C.W. Davis at the steamboat landing. After the railroad line bypassed Jacksonport in the 1870s the town declined. In 1963 restoration began, and two years later the old settlement became a state park, with a few nineteenth century structures and some period items which evoke the early days at Jacksonport.

Jenkins' Ferry Civil War Battle Site

The Red River Campaign. At Jenkins' Ferry occurred the third and last of the three major episodes in the Red River Campaign in Arkansas. After the War broke out, a shortage of cotton developed in the north. To remedy the deficiency, the Union devised a plan to enter the Red River in Louisiana and, along with a unit pushing south from Little Rock, to invade Texas where cotton could be grown to supply northern textile mills. Only in 1864 was the plan finally activated. On March 23 General Frederick Steele's troops left Little Rock to rendezvous with General Nathaniel Banks' forces in the Red River region of Louisiana to begin the invasion of Texas. Steele encountered Confederate resistance at Prairie De Ann, at Camden, at Poison Spring on April 18, and at Marks' Mill on April 25 (see the entries for those four places) before finally beginning his retreat toward Little Rock, on April 30 crossing the Saline River at Jenkins' Ferry.

Jenkins' Ferry. After losing most of his supplies at Poison Spring and Marks' Mill, Steele decided to retreat to Little Rock. His troops left Camden on April 26 and three days later reached Leola (then called Sandy Springs). Heavy rains had swollen the Saline River, which Steele's forces crossed on a rubber pontoon bridge. The morning of April 30 the Confederates attacked along the Federal line. Steele defended as his men crossed the river, then his troops continued on to Little Rock, arriving there on May 3. The unsuccessful Red River Campaign proved costly; Steele lost 635 wagons,

2,500 horses and mules, and suffered 2,750 casualties. Of the 4,000 men at Jenkins' Ferry, some 800 were killed or wounded. Exhibits and explanatory plaques at the site recall the episode, while a monument honors Confederate soldiers who died "for the cause."

Lake Village

Ditch Bayou. In a early June 1864 Confederate soldiers defended their positions against some 10,000 Union attackers, sent to remove the pesky Southerners who harassed Northern boats on the Mississippi River.

Little Rock

Old State House. A series of displays entitled "The Arkansas History Exhibits" in the elegant 1836 classic-style former capitol (parts of it were completed later) includes a section on "The Devastation of the Civil War and Reconstruction." The Arkansas secession convention met in May 1861 at the Old State House, from which the state's Confederate government fled when Union troops arrived to occupy Little Rock in September 1863.

Mount Holly Cemetery. Many Arkansas notables, including five Confederate generals, repose at the burial ground. At one grave lies David O. Dodd, a seventeen year old Arkansas youth hanged as a spy by Union military authorities in January 1864. Known as the "Boy Martyr of the Confederacy," Dodd refused an offer to live if he would reveal the identity of the person who had described to him the Union defenses in Little Rock.

Philander Smith College. Founded in 1877, the school was established to provide educational opportunities for freed slaves.

MacArthur Park. The 1838 Old Arsenal Building, in which General Douglas MacArthur was born, now houses the Museum of Science and History. The park occupies land acquired in 1836 by the U.S. government for a military post. The Confederates seized the base when the War broke out, and when they abandoned

Little Rock in 1863 the Southerners tried to burn the arsenal, which survived the attempt.

Lonoke

Courthouse. On the grounds of the 1926 red brick Lonoke County Courthouse stands a monument to Lee and a vintage cannon.

Marianna

Marianna-Lee County Museum. The museum houses War relics.

Marshall

Searcy County Museum. The museum, which occupies the 1902 former city jail, includes War artifacts.

Marks' Mill Battle Site

At Marks' Mill, located near the village of New Edinburg, occurred the second of three major encounters during the Red River Campaign in Arkansas. On April 25 a Confederate force of 2,500 men attacked a Union wagon train of 240 vehicles and some 1,600 men. During the five hour battle, the Southerners captured the entire convoy, along with most of the enemy soldiers and 1,500 horses and mules. Deprived of food and ammunition after the attacks on Union supply convoys at Poison Spring and Marks' Mill, Steele's forces were forced to retreat back toward Little Rock.

Monticello

The last known military action of the War occurred near Monticello on May 24, 1865, more than six weeks after Lee's surrender at Appomattox on April 9.

North Little Rock

Old Mill. The re-created old-time water powered grist mill was filmed for the opening scene of the movie *Gone with the Wind,* the War era epic.

Old Washington Historic State Park

Hempstead County Courthouse. Following the capture of Little Rock on September 10, 1863, the Confederates moved the seat of government to the 1863 courthouse, where on October 2, 1864, the Arkansas Confederate state government held its last General Assembly session. Meanwhile, back in Little Rock, Isaac Murphy, who cast the lone dissenting note at the secession convention, was elected to serve as the state's Union governor.

Royston House. At the 1846 residence lived lawyer and planter Grandison D. Royston, who was a member of the Confederate House of Representatives.

B.W. Edwards Weapons Museum. A c. 1925 former bank building houses the collection which includes War era firearms and Bowie knives, nicknamed the "Arkansas toothpick." A reconstructed blacksmith shop in the park recalls the original shop where James Black supposedly forged the very first Bowie knife for James Bowie, who designed the weapon.

Pea Ridge National Military Park

More than 750 military encounters occurred in Arkansas. Although most of them involved only skirmishes, ambushes and minor incidents, the March 7-8, 1862, clash at Pea Ridge, with some 26,000 combatants, was the largest battle fought west of the Mississippi. The Union victory at Pea Ridge enabled the North to retain control of Missouri. On March 4 General Earl Van Dorn's 16,000-man force started north from the Fayetteville area with the intention of invading Missouri and capturing St. Louis. In the Pea Ridge area Van Dorn encountered 10,500 Union troops under General Samuel Curtis. Van Dorn mounted a two-pronged attack, during which two of his generals were killed. Southern forces included three regiments of 1,000 Cherokees from the Indian

Territory, now Oklahoma. Pea Ridge was the War's only major battle which included Indian combatants. On the morning of March 8 Curtis counter-attacked, forcing Van Dorn to retreat.

The 4,300 acre park includes a visitor center and twelve viewing points and other sites on a seven mile driving tour around the battlefield area.

Pea Ridge—the largest battlefield west of the Mississippi and the first one west of the river to be designated as a national park—is the most important War site in Arkansas. The state of Arkansas is surveying some lesser known War sites, as yet undeveloped. These sites (not listed in this section) include: Bayou Fourche in Pulaski County; Hill's Plantation in Woodruff County; Canehill in Washington County; Devil's Backbone in Sebastian County; Old River Lake in Chicot County; and Elkins' Ferry in Clark County. For further information: 501-682-1191.

Piggott

Chalk Bluff. War trenches remain at this area east of town.

Pine Bluff

Pine Bluff/Jefferson County Museum. Installed in the restored train depot, the museum includes War exhibits.

University of Arkansas at Pine Bluff. The "Persistence of the Spirit" exhibit traces the history of black Arkansas residents from 1803 to 1986. Photos and memorabilia recall the War era.

The First Shot. Pine Bluff claims that the War's very first shot was fired in the city and not at Charleston, South Carolina. A few days before the shelling of Fort Sumter on April 12, 1861, two Confederate militia companies at Pine Bluff fired a warning shot at a steamboat carrying supplies up the Arkansas River to Federal troops garrisoned at Fort Smith.

Poison Spring Battleground Historic Monument

At the Spring—named after Union soldiers poisoned the water

in an attempt to deter a Confederate force advancing from Camden—occurred the first of three major encounters of the Red River Campaign in Arkansas (for a summary of the campaign, see the entry for Jenkins' Ferry Civil War Battle Site). General Frederick Steele's army included 13,000 soldiers, 9,000 horses and mules, 800 wagons and thirty artillery pieces. To supply this force required an extensive logistical support system. At Poison Spring, about ten miles west of Camden, some 3,100 Confederate troops on April 18, 1864, attacked a Federal supply train of 198 wagons. The Southerners captured 170 of the wagons, burned the others and routed the Union units.

Prairie De Ann

Earthen embankments recall the early April 1864 encounter when General Frederick Steele, advancing from Little Rock to join General Nathaniel Banks for the invasion of Texas, spent a day and a half overcoming a Confederate defensive unit.

Prairie Grove Battlefield State Park

On December 7, 1862, General Thomas C. Hindman led 11,000 Arkansas Confederate troops into combat against some 7,000 Union soldiers near Prairie Grove Church. After Union troops withdrew, the Confederates, short of ammunition, also retired, leaving the outcome of the encounter indecisive. Federal forces, however, soon took control of northern Arkansas.

Hindman Hall Museum houses a diorama of the battle, War artifacts, and displays on the life of a soldier, while a driving tour and a one mile trail take visitors through the 130 acre park, which includes a nineteenth century museum village. Among the buildings is the Morrow House (moved to the park from Cove Creek), where Confederate General Sterling Price stayed prior to the Battle of Pea Ridge and where Hindman stayed the night before the Battle of Prairie Grove. The residence now houses an exhibit on the effect of the War on Ozark culture.

Prescott

Nevada County Depot Museum. The old train depot houses a museum which includes War relics from the Prairie De Ann battlefield.

Scott

Plantation Agricultural Museum. The museum recalls the antebellum way of life which the South fought to preserve. Exhibits trace the story of cotton growing and the plantation culture in Arkansas from the pre-War years, starting in 1836, up to World War II.

Sheridan

Grant County Museum. Located in a one story wood building with a porch front like an old general store, the museum houses War relics from the battlefield at Jenkins' Ferry.

Both Grant County, formed during the Reconstruction era, and the county seat of Sheridan were named for Union generals—Ulysses S. Grant and Phillip Sheridan. Area residents seeking their own county thought their petition would stand a better chance of approval by Federal authorities with Union heroes' names for the county and its seat.

Springdale

Shiloh Museum. The museum, established by the city in 1965 and named for the mid-nineteenth century settlement which became Springdale, includes extensive archives on regional history and the historical collections of six counties. A new facility houses some of the materials. The museum sponsors War encampments and re-enactments of battles.

St. Charles

On June 17, 1862, at St. Charles occurred the War's single most destructive shot when a Confederate cannonball hit a boiler of the

Mound City on the White River and touched off a massive explosion which killed nearly 150 Union soldiers. A sign outside town bears a cannon image, which alludes to the episode.

Texarkana

Confederate Monument. The memorial statue, carved in Italy and installed in 1918, commemorates not only Confederate soldiers but also their mothers.

Van Buren

Main Street. Troops of the Blue and of the Gray fought along the street and at the waterfront in the warehouse district, which burned to the ground during the encounter. The Union unleashed the attack in an attempt to block Confederate access to Indian allies in the area. More recently, the turn-of-the-century buildings lining Main Street served to portray Gettysburg and Vicksburg in the TV mini-series "The Blue and the Gray."

Fairview Cemetery. Confederate soldiers killed during the Van Buren battle repose in the burial ground.

War Eagle Mill

A latter-day (1973) reproduction of an 1873 water-powered grist mill recall the site's earlier mill (c. 1840), which a Confederate general burned to prevent its capture and use by Federal forces.

White Oak Lake State Park

Near this area General Frederick Steele's troops camped prior to occupying Camden.

Chapter IV

Civil War Sites in Northern Areas

Illinois

Alton

Lincoln-Douglas. A pink granite marker near the Mississippi indicates the site of the seventh and last debate, held October 15, 1858, between the two candidates for the U.S. Senate. The series of famous debates, arranged in Bement (see that entry), took place from August to October 1858 at Ottawa, Freeport, Jonesboro, Charleston, Galesburg and Quincy (see those entries), concluding at Alton. Although the immediate issue was the Senate election, underlying the debates were the questions of slavery and the future of the Union. Lincoln lost the election, but he became nationally known through the debates.

Lovejoy Monument. A 93-foot-high granite pillar, the state's tallest monument (1897), honors Elijah Lovejoy, the fervent abolitionist and editor killed November 7, 1837. Nearby is Lovejoy's grave, while the *Alton Telegraph* office in town displays part of the press an angry pro-slavery mob threw into the Mississippi.

Alton Museum of History and Art. The museum contains a section on Lovejoy and a Lincoln Room with exhibits on the debate.

State Prison. During the War, Illinois's first state prison (1833), located at the corner of Broadway and Williams, was reopened to hold captured Confederate soldiers.

Confederate Soldiers' Cemetery. A monument in North Alton lists names of the captives who died in the prison. Some of the estimated 1354 dead lie in the cemetery, while others were buried on "Smallpox Island" in the Mississippi where a hospital and a cemetery operated during the 1863 epidemic.

Batavia

Depot Museum. The restored 1855 train depot includes the Mary Todd Lincoln Room with Mrs. Lincoln's furniture.

Belvidere

Cemetery. At the cemetery reposes Stephen A. Hurlbut, first national commander of the Grand Army of the Republic.

Bement

Bryant Cottage. At the 1856 cottage, owned by a cousin of poet William Cullen Bryant, Lincoln and Douglas met on July 29, 1858, to make arrangements for the seven later famous debates between the two Senate candidates.

Bloomington

"Lost Speech." A marker commemorates Lincoln's 1856 extemporaneous anti-secession speech to the meeting at which the state Republican party was organized. The speech, whose content no one recorded, set the theme for Lincoln's political career and made him a prominent figure in the newly organized party.

McLean County Historical Society Museum. The museum includes materials pertaining to the War and to Lincoln.

Clover Lawn. At the house lived David Davis, who Lincoln appointed to the U.S. Supreme Court and who later served as the assassinated president's executor.

Soldiers' Monument. The monument honors McLean County's dead in all wars prior to World War I.

Bryon

Soldiers' Memorial. The 1866 monument was Illinois's first memorial to War soldiers.

Cairo

Ulysses S. Grant. When the guns boomed during the War so did Cairo. In September 1861 Grant established his headquarters in the city and there gathered troops for the advance into the South, which began in early February 1862. During the War an estimated one million Union troops passed through Cairo, which served as headquarters for the Union river fleet. At the corner of Ohio and 2d Streets stood the St. Charles Hotel where Grant occupied room 215, from which he could observe his troops and flotilla.

Fort Defiance. By action of accretion, the Mississippi and the Ohio Rivers have added about a mile to the southern tip of Illinois since the War. In September 1861 the Union occupied Fort Defiance near the then existing confluence point. Fort Defiance is now the name of a park—no fort exists there—at the meeting point of the two great rivers. From the fort Grant launched his surprise flanking movement, thrusting westward into Tennessee rather than, as expected, advancing down the Mississippi to Memphis. In February 1862 Grant captured Forts Henry and Donelson (see those entries in the Tennessee section) and then clashed with the Confederates at the bloody Battle of Shiloh (see that entry).

Tigress. In a small park stands the flagpole from the Union boat *Tigress,* which in April 1862 carried Grant up the Tennessee River to the Battle of Shiloh. A year later, when the vessel sank while attempting to run the Confederate shore batteries at Vicksburg, the crew salvaged the flagpole and returned it to Cairo.

Cairo Public Library. The Library houses not only books but also history displays, some of which recall the War era.

Church of the Redeemer. The church bell, supposedly cast from one thousand silver dollars, once hung on the War transport ship *James Montgomery*, sunk in 1861.

Carbondale

Woodlawn Cemetery. A bronze marker at the entrance to the cemetery claims that the first organized observance of Decoration Day took place there when a group of War veterans held a memorial service on April 29, 1866.

Charleston

Lincoln-Douglas. A marker at the fairgrounds on the west side of town indicates the site of the fourth debate, held September 8, 1858.

Courthouse Square. A riot involving Southern sympathizers and Union soldiers broke out in the square in March 1864.

Dennis Hanks Grave. While attending the Edgar County fair in Paris, Illinois, in 1892 Lincoln's cousin and boyhood chum was run down and killed by a team of horses.

Moore Home State Historic Site. Nine miles south of Charleston lies the property where Lincoln's stepmother and her daughter lived.

Lincoln Log Cabin State Historic Site. A mile south of the Moore house stands the reconstructed 1837 log cabin built by Lincoln's father, Thomas, who reposes at the nearby Shiloh Cemetery along with Sarah Bush Lincoln, his wife and the president's stepmother.

Chicago

Chicago Historical Society. A major gallery devoted to Lincoln and the War includes the bed on which the president died and tables used for the surrender at Appomattox and for signing the Emancipation Proclamation.

Abraham Lincoln Book Shop. Located at 357 West Chicago

Avenue, the store, established in 1933, offers one of the country's best selections of books and documents on the War and Lincoln.

Stephen A. Douglas. At the eastern end of 35th Street stands a statue of Lincoln's great rival in the pre-War era. The 1879 statue, Chicago's oldest sculptured monument, contains in the base Douglas's tomb. At a nearby site operated Camp Douglas, a War training post and prison.

Oak Woods Cemetery. In the southwest corner repose some 6000 Confederate soldiers who died while being held prisoner at Camp Douglas. Bronze tablets list the names and units of 4275 deceased, and a bronze statue of a grieving infantryman tops a granite pillar.

Grant and Lincoln Parks. A statue of Grant stands in Lincoln Park, and also an 1887 statue of Lincoln by Augustus Saint-Gaudens. In Grant Park is another statue of Lincoln by Saint-Gaudens as well as his equestrian statue of Union general John A. Logan.

Fort Sheridan. Located in Highwood, a northern suburb of Chicago, the National Historic Landmark includes a museum of military history with exhibits on the War. On Sheridan Road near Lake Shore Drive stands a statue by Gutzon Borglum of Union general Philip Sheridan, shown mounted on his galloping stallion.

Underground Railroad. A plaque at 9955 South Verley Avenue notes Chicago's role in the network of safe houses used by slaves to escape to the North.

Clinton

Lincoln Statue. The statue at Courthouse Square commemorates Lincoln's supposed comment addressed to Douglas on July 27, 1858: "You can fool all the people part of the time and part of the people all of the time, but you cannot fool all the people all the time." While opposing Douglas in an Eighth Judicial Circuit railroad case at Clinton, Lincoln first met George B. McClellan, an Illinois Central engineer who the president later appointed to head the Union armies.

Danville

Lamon House. In Danville lived Ward Hill Lamon, Lincoln's confidant and sometime bodyguard during the War.

Decatur

Lincoln Statutes. A statue at Milliken University depicts young Lincoln, barefoot and beardless and lacking the craggy, haggard look of the War years. Other statues in town stand in front of the courthouse and at the Macon County Building, the latter depicting "Lincoln the Lawyer."

Wigwam Convention Hall. At 200 East Main stood the hall where in May 1860 the Illinois Republican convention met to decide which presidential candidate to support. Delegates voted to "use all honourable means to secure" Lincoln's nomination. At the convention, Lincoln first received the nickname "the Railsplitter."

Lincoln Trail Homestead State Park. The park features a replica of the log cabin Lincoln and his father built when they moved to Illinois in 1830.

Lincoln Square. Here Lincoln practiced law and delivered his first political speeches.

Lincoln Log Cabin Courthouse. In Fairview Park is a reproduction of the courthouse where in 1838 Lincoln won his first major case. Douglas represented the opposing side.

Elkhart

Richard J. Oglesby. Elkhart is the home town and burial site (1899) of the three-time Illinois governor, a War general and friend of Lincoln who was at the president's bedside when he died.

Freeport

Lincoln-Douglas. A memorial boulder marks the site of the second debate, held August 27, 1858.

War Monument. On the courthouse lawn stands the 1869 monument, which depicts four War military figures.

Galena

Ulysses S. Grant. When the War began Grant was living in Galena working as a clerk in his father's leather store at 120 South Main Street. Grant, his wife and four children occupied a modest brick house on Quality Hill. A sign in the yard notes: "From this home Captain Ulysses S. Grant, a citizen of Galena, Illinois, went to the Civil War, May 1861." When Grant returned to Galena after the War some of the townspeople gave him a spacious house, now a State Historic Site. The house, Grant's home residence during his two terms as president, contains original furnishings and Grant family items.

Grant Park. At the park by the Galena River stands the 1892 statue "Grant Our Citizen." Nearby is a War monument.

Galena-Jo Daviess County History Museum. The museum includes War clothes and other era items, among them Thomas Nast's famous painting "Peace in Union" picturing Lee's surrender to Grant at Appomattox. The painting also depicts two of the nine Union generals from Galena.

Rawlins House. At 515 Hill Street lived John A. Rawlins, one of Galena's generals. He helped Grant organize the 12th Illinois Infantry Regiment, and later became Grant's aide. After Grant entered the White House he appointed Rawlins secretary of war. Shortly afterward, he died at age thirty-seven.

Smith House. Another local general, John E. Smith, lived at 801 South Bench. A jeweler and silversmith, Smith organized the "Lead Mine Regiment," an infantry unit so nicknamed for the mines in the area. Jasper Maltby, who helped Smith organize the regiment, also served as a Union general. It was Maltby who invented the telescopic sight for rifles.

U.S. Custom House and Post Office. Ely S. Parker supervised the building of the 1857 government building. A Seneca Indian, Parker served as captain of an engineer unit under John E. Smith and later became a general. As a member of Grant's staff, Parker was present at the surrender at Appomattox.

Washbourne House State Historic Site. Elihu Washbourne, a mentor for Grant, served in Congress from 1852 to 1869 and later became secretary of state. Grant drilled his volunteer troops on the lawn of the house before marching them off to the War.

De Soto Hotel. In 1856 Lincoln spoke from the balcony of the hotel, used by Grant in 1868 as his campaign headquarters.

First Methodist Church. A plaque at the 1857 church marks the Grant family pew.

Illinois Central Depot. Now the tourist center, the 1857 depot was where Grant arrived home after the War and from where he departed for Washington as president-elect.

Galesburg

Knox College. Old Main is the only remaining building associated with one of the seven Lincoln-Douglas debates. Some 20,000 people, the largest crowd in the series, attended the October 7, 1858, event, held on a platform just outside Old Main. The Knox College Library houses the Smith Collection of War books.

Carl Sandburg State Historic Site. A plaque posted at Knox College commemorating the debate supposedly sparked in young Sandburg, a local resident, an interest in Lincoln which eventually led to Sandburg's monumental biography of the president. The small house where young Sandburg lived (before the War a stop on the Underground Railroad) recalls the Lincoln biographer's early days in Galesburg.

"Mother" Bickerdyke. A monument on the courthouse lawn bears Sherman's compliment that "she outranks me," a comment offered in praise of Mary Bickerdyke's organization of nursing services during the War. She reposes at the Linwood Cemetery in Galesburg.

Giant City State Park

Knights of the Golden Circle. Southern Illinois extends farther south than most of Virginia and Kentucky. During the War, citizens of the region agitated to establish the area as a separate state aligned with the Confederacy. Some of the Southern sympathizers joined the Knights, a secret Confederate spying organization whose area headquarters were in the rocky terrain now part of the park. On one rock formation a bodyguard of Jefferson Davis scratched the guard's name in February 1862.

Hanover

At the beginning of the War Grant traveled from nearby Galena to deliver his first public address to young army recruits in Hanover.

Jacksonville

Illinois College. Settled by New Englanders, Jacksonville was a center of abolitionist sentiment and a main stop on the Underground Railroad. Edward Beecher, brother of Harriet Beecher Stowe, served as first president of the college (established 1829), whose first graduating class (1835) included future Illinois War governor Richard Yates. An organization at the college sponsored Lincoln's February 11, 1859, lecture in Jacksonville.

Stephen A. Douglas. Lincoln's rival began the practice of law in Jacksonville in 1834. After making an inspiring speech in the town to disheartened Democrats the diminutive Douglas was given his nickname, "The Little Giant."

Monuments. In the square stands a War memorial; another War monument stands in East Cemetery; a marker at the fairgrounds indicates where Grant's troops camped on the way to Missouri;

plaques on East State Street and at the American Legion Home recall Union general Benjamin Grierson, founder of a well known band, who in 1863 led a cavalry raid into Mississippi, advancing 600 miles between April 17 and May 2.

Jonesboro

Lincoln-Douglas. A marker at the north edge of town indicates the site of the third debate, held September 15, 1858.

Junction

Old Slave House. According to tradition, at the 1834 house lived slaves who worked at the nearby Equality Salt Wells. Although the Northwest Ordinance prohibited slavery, making Illinois a free state, special provisions permitted exceptions at the saline area, which was thus the only part of Illinois where slavery legally existed.

Lewistown

Ross Mansion. Local lore relates that Union supporters aimed a cannon at the house, supposedly designed by a Southern sympathizer.

Lincoln Pillars. At the cemetery two pillars removed from the old courthouse serve as a memorial to dead soldiers. Lincoln stood between the pillars during his August 17, 1858, speech at the courthouse.

Lincoln

Lincoln in Lincoln. Lincoln himself showed up on August 27, 1853, to christen the new town, the first in the nation to bear his name, with watermelon juice. At the old depot Lincoln's funeral train halted briefly at sunrise May 3, 1865.

Postville Courthouse State Historic Site. At the courthouse Lincoln received the nickname "Honest Abe" for his refusal to defend a client he deemed guilty. The present building is a replica of the original 1841 structure now at Greenfield Village in Detroit.

Lincoln College. A statue depicts Lincoln as a studious youth, while the college library houses a Lincoln museum.

Rustic Tavern. At the old tavern a band of ne'er-do-wells hatched a plot to rob Lincoln's grave in Springfield and ransom the body.

Mattoon

Depot. As recalled by a tablet at the Illinois Central Depot, in June 1861 Grant mustered the 21st Illinois Infantry into service here.

Metamora

Metamora Courthouse State Historic Site. The 1844 Southern Colonial-style structure is one of two surviving Illinois Eighth Judicial Circuit courthouses where Lincoln practiced law. The other is at Mt. Pulaski (entry below). Lawyers who traveled the circuit in the 1840s included Douglas, Robert Ingersoll, famous agnostic of the era, and Adlai Stevenson, U.S. vice president under Cleveland.

Metropolis

Fort Massac State Park. During the War Northern troops occupied the outpost by the Ohio River.

Mt. Pulaski

Mt. Pulaski Courthouse State Historic Site. The 1848 Greek Revival-style structure is one of two surviving Illinois Eighth Circuit courthouses where Lincoln appeared in cases. The other is at Metamora.

Morris

Grundy County Courthouse. A memorial notes the county's role in the summer 1863 siege of Vicksburg.

Mound City

National Cemetery. Nearly 5000 soldiers, more than half of them unknown, from both armies repose at the burial ground near Mound City. Other graves include those of some fifty nurses who ministered to the 2300 wounded brought after the Battle of Shiloh to the Federal naval hospital in Mound City.

Naval Hospital. The southern section of a still standing brick building by the Ohio River was converted in 1861 to the largest naval hospital on the western rivers.

Marine Ways. During the War Mound City served as the nerve center for the Western Rivers Fleet. At Marine Ways, a construction and repair yard, 1500 workers built three gunboats and converted steamboats into fighting vessels. A commercial river operation still exists at the Marine Ways site.

Murphysboro

John A. Logan. An equestrian statue and the house where Logan lived recall the Union general, whose oratory persuaded southern Illinois, filled with Confederate sympathizers, to support the Northern cause.

Naperville

War Monument. The Grand Army of the Republic installed the monument honoring War soldiers in 1870.

New Burnside

The village, established in 1872 when the Big Four Railroad was built through the area, took its name from Union general Ambrose E. Burnside (see also the Burnside, Kentucky, entry), president of the line.

New Salem

Lincoln's New Salem State Historic Site. This reconstruction of the village where Lincoln lived from 1831 to 1837 includes one original building, the Onstott Cooper Shop, along with twenty-two reproductions of stores, houses, mills and other structures. Antique furnishings and a museum with Lincoln items recall the era.

Normal

Hovey House. Union officer Charles E. Hovey commanded an Illinois unit, nicknamed the "Brain Regiment," comprised mainly of students and professors from Illinois State Normal University. Although Hovey bravely continued his command after his arm was severely wounded during a battle in Arkansas, he failed to win Senate confirmation as a general officer.

Olney

The Olney Times issue for November 1, 1858, published a headline, "For President in 1860, Abraham Lincoln of Illinois." This was supposedly the first newspaper endorsement for the office Lincoln received.

Oregon

Soldiers' Monument. The 1916 monument, by well known Illinois sculptor Lorado Taft, stands on the courthouse lawn.

Ottawa

Lincoln-Douglas. A boulder in Washington Park marks the site where the first debate took place, August 21, 1858. The three hour event attracted a crowd twice as big as the town's population of 5000.

Reddick Mansion. The twenty-two room house, built the year after the debate, served as a stop on the Underground Railroad.

Peoria

Courthouse. A plaque at the portico of the courthouse recalls Lincoln's October 16, 1854, speech, a rebuttal to a long address delivered by Douglas. In his remarks Lincoln for the first time, it is believed, publicly denounced slavery, so introducing a theme which he developed over the years leading to the War.

Petersburg

Rosehill Cemetery. At the cemetery reposes Dr. Benjamin F. Stephenson, founder of the Grand Army of the Republic and its first adjutant general.

Pittsfield

John Hay. The future private secretary to Lincoln during the War (see the Warsaw entry) lived in Pittsfield for two years as a student.

John G. Nicolay. Nicolay, of the *Free Press* newspaper, was supposedly the first person to suggest Lincoln for the presidency. When Lincoln gained the office, he appointed the former journalist as a private secretary.

Princeton

Owen Lovejoy Homestead. In the restored fifteen room 1838 house lived the abolitionist preacher, who ran a station on the Underground Railroad. The brother of martyred editor Elijah Lovejoy (see the Alton entry), Lovejoy served five terms in the U.S. House, where he introduced the Emancipation Proclamation bill to Congress.

Bryant House. The Underground Railroad also operated a station at the house of John Bryant, delegate to the 1860 convention at which Lincoln was nominated for the presidency.

Quincy

Lincoln-Douglas. A bronze bas relief in Washington Park marks where the sixth debate took place on October 13, 1858. Quotations on the monument note Lincoln's point that slavery "is a wrong" and Douglas's comment that slave owners "are civilized men."

Historical Society of Quincy and Adams County. The 1830s mansion of John Wood, governor of Illinois, includes items from the War era.

All Wars Museum. A soldier figure clad in War garb stands on guard near the museum, which includes items from the conflict.

Rock Island

Arsenal. In 1862 the government established on an island in the Mississippi the Federal Arsenal, which still functions. Dr. John Emerson, a doctor for two years at a previous garrison on the island, brought with him from St. Louis Dred Scott, the slave who based his later suit for freedom on his residence in a free state (see the Old Courthouse entry in the St. Louis, Missouri, listing).

Confederate Cemetery. At the cemetery on Arsenal Island repose nearly 2000 Southerners who died in the nearby prison camp.

Prison. A marker on the island indicates the site of the prison, which held more than 12,000 captured Confederate soldiers.

Chippiannock Cemetery. An elaborate Celtic cross carved by the father of well known sculptor Alexander Calder memorializes War naval officer W.H. Harte, buried elsewhere.

Rosiclare

Illinois Iron Furnace. Iron was produced during the War at the fifty-two foot high restored charcoal-fired furnace listed on the National Register.

Salem

James S. Martin. At 709 Main Street lived the Union general and later U.S. Senator.

Springfield

Lincoln's Tomb State Historic Site. Small statues in the tomb building depict various periods of Lincoln's life. The president, his wife and three sons repose here; Robert Todd Lincoln, the fourth son, is buried at Arlington National Cemetery.

Lincoln Home National Historic Site. Lincoln family items furnish the house, where he lived for seventeen years.

Depot. At the train depot Lincoln noted his "feeling of sadness at this parting" as he left Springfield on February 11, 1861, for Washington and the White House.

Lincoln-Herndon Building. The 1840 building contains exhibits and furnishings from the time when Lincoln practiced law there (1843 to 1852) with William Herndon, his future biographer.

State Historical Society. The Society's library houses one of the nations's largest collections of Lincoln material: some 10,000 manuscripts, books and documents. The Lincoln Room contains family memorabilia.

State Capitol. Paintings and sculpture depicting such War figures as Lincoln, Douglas and Grant embellish the state house.

Old State Capitol. On display is one of the five surviving copies of the Gettysburg Address in Lincoln's own handwriting. At Representative Hall upstairs Lincoln delivered the famous "A house divided against itself cannot stand" speech in June 1858. Seven years later, on May 3-4, 1865, the president's body lay in state in the chamber.

First Presbyterian Church. A marker designates the Lincoln family pew.

Marine Bank. On display is the ledger page showing Lincoln's account at the bank.

Grand Army of the Republic Memorial Museum. The museum features displays devoted to the War.

Daughters of Union Veterans of the Civil War. The national headquarters houses books, documents and memorabilia from the War.

Camp Butler National Cemetery. Located east of Springfield, the cemetery, opened in 1862, occupies in part a site used during the War as a training camp and prison. About one-third of the Union troops from Illinois were inducted and trained at the camp. At the cemetery are buried 1642 soldiers from both armies.

Thebes

Courthouse. According to local legend, slave Dred Scott was held captive in the basement of the 1848 former Alexander County courthouse.

Warsaw

John Hay. At 185-187 Clay (west side) stands the 1841 double house where Hay, son of a local physician, lived as a boy. Hay served as Lincoln's private secretary during the War, and later co-authored a ten volume biography of the president. He was at Lincoln's bedside when the president died (see also Salem, Indiana).

West Dundee

Allan Pinkerton. Pinkerton, the nation's first "private eye," emigrated from Scotland to West Dundee in 1843. Pinkerton's abolitionist activities in the area attracted the attention of Lincoln, who chose him to organize and head the Union army's Secret Service, a forerunner of U.S. Secret Service. Pinkerton's vigilance helped thwart an assassination plot against Lincoln in Baltimore.

Winchester

Douglas Monument. In the square stands a life-size bronze of Lincoln's opponent. Douglas taught school and began his legal career in the town in 1833-1834.

Lincoln Speech. A boulder marks where Lincoln delivered his first speech on the Kansas-Nebraska issue, the 1854 bill sponsored by Douglas allowing the new territories in the West the option to choose to allow or prohibit slavery.

Indiana

Bedford

Lawrence County Historical Museum. Displays include War items.

Bloomington

Lilly Library of Indiana University. The Lincoln Room houses part of the Lincoln Collection, which includes more than 5000 books and 3000 manuscripts relating to the president. Four portraits and a bronze bust of Lincoln decorate the room; furnishings include a desk from the Springfield, Illinois, law office of Stephen T. Logan, Lincoln's law partner from 1841 to 1844.

Centerville

War governor Oliver P. Morton was born in Centerville, a picturesque village with antique shops occupying the 1830s and 1840s buildings which evoke a pre-War Midwestern hamlet.

Corydon

Battle of Corydon. A mile south of Corydon—one-time territorial (1813-16) and state (1816-24) capital—lies the site of one of the few battles fought on Northern soil and the only battle in Indiana. On July 9, 1863, General John Hunt Morgan's 2400 Confederate raiders defeated some 400 Corydon Home Guard soldiers.

Morgan's Raiders. Crossing the Ohio from Kentucky, Morgan entered Indiana the night of July 8 at Mackport. After the battle at Corydon he camped near Palmyra to the north, then continued on to Salem (see that entry) and then east through Vienna where he tapped the telegraph and gleaned military dispatches relating to his raids. After proceeding to Lexington, Morgan headed north through Scottsburg to Vernon (see that entry) and then moved on to Dupont and Versailles. After traveling 200 miles through Indiana, Morgan left the state and crossed into Ohio on July 13. Markers in some of the areas Morgan harassed recall his raids across southern Indiana.

Posey House Museum. Displays include War items.

Kintner House Inn. This antique-filled bed and breakfast establishment served as headquarters for a few hours for Morgan during his fighting in the area. While at the house, Morgan was told by a gleeful Miss Sallie Kintner of the Confederate defeat at Gettysburg. One of the inn's bedrooms is named for Morgan. Lincoln's uncle, Josiah Lincoln, was an early day guest at the inn.

Crawfordsville

Lew Wallace Study. Wallace served as a Union general, and as an official in the Lincoln assassination trial. In 1880 he published his famous novel *Ben Hur*. The Study, a National Historic Landmark, built on the grounds of Wallace's home in 1896, contains his memorabilia and papers, including some items connected with his War experience.

Henry S. Lane House. At the 1846 Greek Revival-style mansion, listed on the National Register, lived the Indiana governor and U.S. senator. Lane was instrumental in the nomination of Lincoln for president on the Republican ticket. Objects on display include War memorabilia.

Elkhart

Elkhart County Historical Museum. A collection of military uniforms includes some from the War.

Fort Wayne

Louis A. Warren Lincoln Library and Museum. The facility houses books, paintings and personal items pertaining to Lincoln.

Allen County-Fort Wayne Historical Society Museum. The first of the six historical periods covered by the museum displays includes exhibits on the War.

Fountain City

Levi Coffin State Historic Site. Over 2000 escaped slaves found refuge at the eight-room brick house during the twenty years Quakers Levi and Catharine Coffin lived in the 1839 residence. Coffin, known as the "President of the Underground Railroad," offered the fugitives food, shelter and clothing as the escaped slaves headed north. Coffin appears as the character Simeon Halliday in Harriet Beecher Stowe's *Uncle Tom's Cabin,* the pre-War anti-slavery novel.

French Lick Springs

The famous spa and resort was founded in the 1820s by Dr. William A. Bowles, a Southern sympathizer. To counter the use of French Lick as a station on the Underground Railroad, Bowles organized the Knights of the Golden Circle, a Confederate secret society. Just before the War, Bowles was convicted of treason in a plot to kidnap Governor Morton and sentenced to death. Lincoln, however, commuted the sentence to life imprisonment. After spending the War in a Federal prison in Ohio, Bowles was released and he returned to French Lick where he managed the hotel until his death in 1873.

Lawrenceburg

Vance-Tousey House. In 1818 Samuel C. Vance, for whose wife Mary Lawrence the town was named, completed "the finest mansion between Cincinnati and Louisville." Union general Don Carlos Buell supposedly stayed at the house. An historical marker in town commemorates Lincoln's 1861 visit to Lawrenceburg.

Lincoln Boyhood National Memorial

Memorial. The Memorial includes a visitor center with exhibits; a Living Historical Farm, operated as in the era when the Lincoln family lived in the area from 1816 to 1830; and the grave of Nancy Hanks Lincoln, Abe's mother.

Lincoln State Park. At the nearby park, from mid-June to mid-August, the musical show *Young Abe Lincoln* dramatizes the boy's life in the area where he lived from age seven to twenty-one. The Railsplitter Supper, served before performances, includes gingerbread, said to be Lincoln's favorite dessert. In the 1747 acre park reposes Sarah Lincoln Grisby, the president's sister.

Madison

Lanier Mansion. The stately Ohio River residence, completed in 1844, belonged to financier James F.D. Lanier. When Lincoln requested six regiments from Indiana, Lanier loaned nearly $500,000 to equip the 10,000 troops, and an additional $500,000 for state operating expenses.

Middleton Monument. On Main Street, just east of the Old Jail, stands the War memorial.

Helm House. At 610 Main stands the house occupied during the War by Mary Todd Lincoln's half sister. Mrs. Helm's husband, a Confederate officer, died in the Battle of Chickamauga (see that entry in the Georgia section).

Bright House. The residence at 312 West 3d Street was built in 1837 by Jesse Bright, Senator from Indiana during the War.

Old Shipyards. At the western edge of town on the Ohio operated shipyards where a Union gunboat was built.

New Albany

National Soldiers' Cemetery. Established in 1862, the burial ground includes graves of War veterans.

Anderson School. At the southwest corner of Lafayette and Market Streets stood the Anderson Female Seminary, established in 1841. The future Confederate general and Indiana nemesis John Hunt Morgan attended Anderson Collegiate Institute for Boys, an affiliated school.

Floyd County Museum. Exhibits include the War period.

Salem

John Hay House. A diminutive one story brick building, built as a school in 1824, was the birthplace in 1838 of John Hay, Lincoln's private secretary during the War and author of a biography of the president. The National Historic Site contains period furnishings.

Stevens Memorial Museum. Exhibits at the museum, just steps away from the Hay House, include War items.

Morgan's Raiders. Salem was one of Indiana's few cities which suffered damage during the War. On July 10, 1863, Morgan's Raiders entered Salem and ransacked the town, burning the train depot, destroying tracks and inflicting other damage.

Thomas Rodman. Near Salem was born Rodman, an 1841 West Point graduate who invented the Rodman gun (see Fort Foote, Maryland), a leading field artillery weapon used during the War.

Spartanburg

Union Literary Institute. The two story red brick 1860 building offers a rare surviving example of a War era school established for black children during a time when even many northern states had laws prohibiting integrated schools.

Terre Haute

Soldiers and Sailors Monument. This War memorial, which

depicts four troops and Indiana's War era governor, stands on the site "where soldiers enlisted" during the conflict.

Vernon

Morgan's Raiders. Only at Vernon did Morgan fail to take one of his Indiana targets. More than 2000 Morgan men faced 400 defenders. Their commander stalled the attack by parlaying with Morgan until 600 reinforcements arrived, after which the Confederate general withdrew.

Wabash

Wabash County Historical Museum. The museum includes War artifacts and records.

West Lafayette

Commandant's Residence State Historic Site. The state built the grandiose mansion, once known as the "White House of the Wabash," in 1899 as a home for disabled Union soldiers. Union troop statues guard the entrance to the Residence, which occupies a site on the grounds of the Indiana State Soldier's Home.

Maryland

Aberdeen

U.S. Army Ordnance Museum. The museum, established just after World War I, includes War items.

Annapolis

U.S. Naval Academy Museum. Displays recall the navy's role during the War.

Naval Academy Chapel. The Farragut Window, installed in 1914, shows Admiral David Farragut lashed to the rigging of his flagship, U.S.S. *Hartford*, observing the Battle of Mobile Bay. The upper window depicts an angel showing the way through the mines, the "torpedoes" Farragut damned to advance full steam ahead (see Fort Morgan in the Alabama section).

"Tecumseh." The Indian image, which overlooks the court in front of Bancroft Hall, was the figurehead which adorned the U.S.S. *Delaware*, scuttled at Norfolk to keep the ship out of Confederate hands. The statue, salvaged from the wreck, was given to the Academy in 1866. The class of 1891 recast the original weathered wood figure in bronze to preserve it.

St. John's College. During the War the college served various functions: a prison, a receiving station, and a hospital for Union troops.

Banneker-Douglass Museum. The "Douglass" refers to the famous black abolitionist Frederick Douglass (see the Douglass House entry in the Washington, D.C., section). The museum, housed in the 1876 church of a congregation founded by free blacks in 1804, features black culture in Maryland.

Antietam

Antietam National Battlefield Site. After a victory at Harpers Ferry, then in Virginia, Stonewall Jackson joined Lee's forces at Antietam Creek where the Confederates made their first attempt to move the War into the north. September 17, 1862, proved to be the bloodiest day of the War, with more than 23,000 killed or wounded. An audio-visual program at the visitor center recounts the story of the Confederate defeat and retreat, while more than 200 markers, monuments and maps at the site describe the course of the battle, known also as Sharpsburg. Present during the clash were Clara Barton, who nursed the wounded, and nineteen years later founded the American Red Cross, and future president William McKinley, sergeant in a Union unit from Ohio.

Baltimore

Camden Station. At the 1852 Baltimore and Ohio station, in its day supposedly the world's largest train terminal, Lincoln stopped on his February 22, 1861, pre-inaugural trip from Philadelphia to Washington. Allan Pinkerton (see West Dundee, Illinois), the famous detective, helped thwart a purported plot to kill the president-elect, who passed through the station at 3:30 a.m., a few hours before his scheduled arrival in town.

On April 19, 1861, 220 Union soldiers took refuge in the station after a skirmish with Southern sympathizers which occurred as the 6th Massachusetts Regiment marched across town between two railroad stations.

Front Street Theater. At the building at the northwest corner of Front and Low Streets, Lincoln and Andrew Johnson were nominated on the presidential ticket in June 1864.

Maryland Historical Society. The Confederate Room includes Lee's camp chair, uniforms, and other War items.

Lee and Jackson Statues. In Wyman Park stand the statues depicting the two generals mounted on their horses meeting at Chancellorsville. Dedicated in 1948, this may be the most recent major monument devoted to the conflict.

Confederate Monument. The 1903 monument at Mount Royal Avenue between Lafayette and Mosher Streets memorializes Southern dead.

Confederate Women's Monument. The 1913 monument, at Charles and University, includes bronze figures of a fallen soldier who clutches at a tattered flag while a nurse braces him.

Patterson Park. Union soldiers took over the site for a base they called Fort Washburn. During part of the War a Federal hospital operated in this area.

Fort McHenry. Dungeons at the fort held some of the 6000 War prisoners, while others were confined in guard houses. During the War the fortress served as an infantry post.

Shot Tower. The 215-foot-tall tower was used from its completion in 1828 until 1892 to produce lead shot gun pellets for hunters and the military. Droplets of molten lead fell from a sieve into a pool of water where they cooled into pellets. At the peak of production, the tower turned out 500,000 2.5-pound bags of shot a year.

Federal Hill. During the War the hill, on Warren Avenue near Key Highway, was used as an observation point. In May 1861 General Benjamin Butler, provoked by an attempt to raise the Confederate flag atop the hill, took control of the rise and emplaced there fifty guns.

Baltimore and Ohio Railroad Museum. The nation's largest railroad museum includes such War related exhibits as a boxcar used to haul supplies during the conflict.

Green Mount Cemetery. John Wilkes Booth lies here in obscurity, with no marker to designate his burial site. Among the Confederate and Union generals who repose in the cemetery is Southerner Joseph E. Johnston.

Robert E. Lee Park. The name memorializes the Confederate general, who moved the Army of Northern Virginia into Maryland in August 1862.

Mount Clare Mansion. The handsome 1760 brick house, Baltimore's oldest mansion, was occupied by Union troops.

Morgan State University. Near the center of the campus stands a twelve-foot statue of abolitionist Frederick Douglass. The school was established in 1867, during the post-War era when many of the nation's black schools were founded.

Great Blacks In Wax Museum. One section of the chronological display is devoted to the War. Among the more than one hundred figures is abolitionist Harriet Tubman (see Bucktown).

Orchard Street Cultural Center. The 1832 church building supposedly served as a stop on the Underground Railroad.

Hayfields. Southern agitator John Merryman lived at the house, located in Baltimore County at the northwest corner of highway 145 and U.S. 111 Expressway, at the time he was arrested. A day after the April 19, 1861, riots (see Camden Station above), at which four soldiers and eleven civilians were killed, the railroad bridges north of the city were burned by Southern sympathizers. Merryman, a militia lieutenant, was arrested. Because writs of habeas corpus had been ignored in two other cases, Merryman's lawyer petitioned U.S. Supreme Court Chief Justice Roger B. Taney directly. Taney traveled to Baltimore to issue the writ, ruling that no government official, including the president, could suspend the writ of habeas corpus.

Bel Alton

John Wilkes Booth and his accomplice, David E. Herold, hid in the woods near town while escaping after Lincoln's assassination. Having grown up in the area, Herold was familiar with the roads and terrain. The fugitives escaped across the Potomac at nearby Pope's Creek where a Southern sympathizer sold them a boat for the crossing. For his part in the assassination plot, Herold was hung on July 7, 1865.

Benevola

According to local lore, the owner of a store in this hamlet near Boonsboro painted a large American flag on an outside wall, but he then whitewashed the decoration out on being informed that Confederate forces were approaching the town.

By Beaver Creek, on the outskirts of Benevola, Union general Meade established an Army of the Potomac headquarters where from July 9-14, 1863, he met with his officers to discuss Lincoln's order to attack Lee before the Southerner retreated south of the Potomac.

Boonsboro

Boonsboro Museum of History. The museum displays War artifacts.

Stonewall Jackson. In September 1862 Federal troops almost captured Jackson in the area as he was walking his horse down a road. A Confederate officer shouted orders to a non-existent unit of troops supposedly hiding in the woods, a ruse which scared off the Union men.

Brunswick

Brunswick Museum and Art Gallery. The museum includes War items.

Bucktown

Old Bridge. Confederates used the covered bridge which once spanned the Potomac here to enter Maryland where they cut telegraph lines and the Baltimore and Ohio rail lines. Union generals crossed the river here to advance into Virginia—McClellan after Antietam and Meade after Gettysburg.

Harriet Tubman. A marker indicates the site where the slave was born in 1820. In 1849 she fled to freedom, then returned to the South nineteen times to help slaves escape on the Underground Railroad. During the War Tubman served as a spy and as a scout for the Union.

Chestertown

War Monument. By the Kent County Courthouse stands the 1917 memorial which honors soldiers of both armies. The Union inscription faces north; the Confederate text, south.

Church Hill

St. Luke's Episcopal Church. The small church off highway 213 in Queen Anne County was besieged by Union cavalry in 1861.

Churchville

Tudor Hall. The house—on Tudor Lane off highway 22 a few miles west of Churchville—was the residence of the Maryland Booth family, whose members included Edwin, the famous Shakespearean actor, and John Wilkes, Lincoln's assassin. The Booth Museum at the mansion, now a bed and breakfast establishment, recalls the assassination.

Clarysville

Clarysville Inn. Built to serve travelers on the old National Road, the 1807 brick and stone inn—known as Eight Mile House—served as headquarters for a large Federal hospital camp.

Clinton

Mary Surratt House. Booth stopped at the 1852 tavern and post office after murdering Lincoln. Mary Surratt was hanged on July 7, 1865, along with three co-defendants, for alleged complicity in the assassination plot. She was the first woman executed by the Federal government, which also tried her son, John, who was acquitted as a co-conspirator. After Mary Surratt's hanging the town changed its original name of Surrattsville.

Cumberland

Colonial Manor. The c. 1785 house, now a restaurant, was used as a hospital after a skirmish at nearby Flock's Mill. On the attic wall of the building—originally a tavern on the National Road—appear comments scribbled by the patients.

Dent House. At 118 Green Street lived George and Susanna Dent, whose son Frederick was the first white child born (1786) in Cumberland County. Frederick, whose daughter married Grant, died in the White House.

Rose Hill. The high hill above the Potomac was occupied in June 1861 by Colonel Lew Wallace and his 11th Indiana Zouaves. Wallace ordered Southern sympathizers to his encampment to make them take an oath of allegiance to the Union.

Baltimore Street. At Barnum Hotel, 154 Baltimore, some sixty Confederate cavalry men, members of McNeill's Raiders (see Willow Hall, West Virginia), captured Brevet Major General Kelly on February 21, 1865. At Revere House, number 184, stood a hotel from which the same band abducted General George Crook the same night. Both generals were taken to Richmond and imprisoned. The 6000 Union troops stationed in Cumberland were unaware of the kidnappings.

Washington Street. At 201 stands the 1846 William O. Sprigg house. Union forces evicted the Sprigg family, Southern sympathizers, and Federal officers occupied the house. At 300 stands the 1860s Joseph Shriver house. When the Indiana Zouaves occupied Cumberland during the War, Shriver advanced wages to the soldiers after the Union army failed to pay the men. At 501 stands the c. 1890 house of Judge Hunter Boyd, an honorary pallbearer at Lee's funeral.

Easton

Slave Market. The market operated on Washington Street next to the courthouse.

Franklin Buchanan. On the south bank of the Miles River west of Easton stood The Rest where Admiral Buchanan, the ranking officer of the Confederate navy, lived. His distinguished career during the War included commanding the *Merrimac* and also at the Battle of Mobile Bay. When Buchanan died at the Rest in 1874 obituaries observed that he had experienced more varied sea service than anyone else in the navy. Buchanan is buried at the cemetery at Wye House, also near the Miles River some fifteen miles northwest of Easton.

Foxley Hall. At the three story brick c. 1794 building lived Confederate colonel Oswald Tilghman.

Fort Foote

The 1863 post, in Prince George's County off highway 414, remains in a good state of preservation. On the grounds stand two fifteen-inch Rodman guns (see the Thomas Rodman entry at Salem, Indiana).

Fort Frederick State Park

The last remaining British stone fort in America (1756) saw

service during the War when Union units occupied the post to guard the nearby Baltimore and Ohio Railroad and the Chesapeake and Ohio Canal.

Fort Washington

George Washington chose the site, on the Potomac opposite Mount Vernon, for the first fort built to defend the capital. The present fort—erected between 1815 and 1824 to replace the original 1809 installation, destroyed by the British in 1814—served to protect Washington at the beginning of the War. After attack by water became less of a threat, the fort's importance declined. In 1864 Fort Foote, also on the Potomac in Maryland, was built with earthen embankments to defend against the new rifled cannons, so making Fort Washington obsolete. The National Park Service administers the facility, abandoned in 1872 but still splendidly preserved.

Frederick

Monocacy Battlefield. On July 9, 1864, Union general Lew Wallace's 5000 troops delayed for twenty-four hours 23,000 Confederates led by General Jubal Early. The delay allowed Grant to reinforce Washington and block the Southerners from capturing the capital. Monuments at the battlefield site, three miles south of Frederick, recall the encounter.

Barbara Fritchie House and Museum. The present house was reconstructed in 1927 as a replica of the original residence, torn down in 1867. The house, which contains Fritchie family items, evokes the incident when the ninety-five-year-old Union activist supposedly defiantly waved the American flag as Confederate troops marched by, a display of patriotism celebrated in John Greenleaf Whittier's famous poem about the episode.

Kemp Hall. The only time the Maryland General Assembly ever met outside Annapolis occurred in April 1861 when a debate on secession took place at the three-story brick hall. The minority

Union faction delayed a vote until Federal troops arrived to arrest the secessionists.

City Hall. On July 9, 1864, just before the Battle of Monocacy, Confederate general Jubal Early met at the city hall with town officials to exact a ransom of $200,000, financed by a bond issue paid off only in 1970.

Taney House and Museum. Roger B. Taney, U.S. Supreme Court Chief Justice before, during and after the War, administered the oath of office to Lincoln (and six other presidents as well). Taney also wrote the Dred Scott decision (see the Old Courthouse entry in the St. Louis, Missouri, listing). The museum includes items relating to Taney, to his brother-in-law, Francis Scott Key, author of the "Star Spangled Banner," and to Lincoln.

Frederick County Historical Society Museum. Located in the Baltzell Mansion, the museum includes displays on Taney.

Hessian Barracks. The barracks, on the grounds of the Maryland State School for the Deaf, were used during the War as a hospital.

Courthouse Square. Lincoln addressed townspeople from the steps of 119 Record Street in October 1862 after visiting Antietam battlefield.

Ramsey House. Lincoln visited General George L. Hartsuff while the officer was recovering at the house from a wound suffered at Antietam.

Evangelical and Reformed Church. On the Sunday before the battle of Antietam Stonewall Jackson napped during services at the church as the minister preached on the need to support the Union cause. Barbara Fritchie belonged to the congregation.

Evangelical and Lutheran Church. The sanctuary served as a hospital during the War, with the wounded laid out on a surface atop the pews.

Winchester Hall. A hospital was installed in the hall during the War.

Mount Olivet Cemetery. Graves include those of Barbara Fritchie and of 875 Confederate soldiers killed at South Mountain,

Antietam and Monocacy. Francis Scott Key also reposes at the cemetery.

Dahlgren Chapel. The widow of John A. Dahlgren, commander of the Washington Navy Yards during the War, built the chapel, located on U.S. highway 40 atop South Mountain.

Gathland State Park

A stone arch monument honoring War reporters stands on a site at the southern end of South Mountain formerly owned by George Townsend, a correspondent of the era. The visitor center houses War papers.

Glen Echo

Clara Barton National Historic Site. During the War Barton, founder of the American Red Cross, tended to wounded at the Second Battle of Manassas, Antietam, the Wilderness, Fredericksburg and Spotsylvania. In 1897 Barton moved into the house—the first permanent headquarters of the Red Cross—which contains some of her furniture and personal possessions.

Cabin John Bridge. In the same area stood the span, a 220-foot-long single masonry arch built between 1857 and 1863. The bridge was originally named for President Franklin Pierce and the Secretary of War, Jefferson Davis, but officials deleted the latter's name after he became president of the Confederacy. The installation now forms part of the Washington, D.C., water system.

Hagerstown

Miller House Museum. The Washington County Historical Society museum includes War artifacts.

Rose Hill Cemetery. An 1877 statue of "Hope" marks graves of some 2000 Confederate soldiers who died at Antietam and South Mountain.

Zion Reformed Church. Union general George Custer used the bell tower of the 1774 church as an observation post until enemy fire forced him to flee from the perch.

Mt. Prospect. A few days after the September 17-18, 1862, Battle of Antietam Mrs. Howard Kennedy watched as a wounded Union officer collapsed near Mt. Prospect house. She took the casualty in and cared for the officer, who was Oliver Wendell Holmes, Jr., later a U.S. Supreme Court justice.

In July 1863 Confederate general John McCausland entered Hagerstown with 1500 men and demanded $20,000 and 20,000 complete sets of clothes. The townspeople handed over all of the money but filled only part of the clothes order.

Hancock

St. Thomas Episcopal Church. In 1861 and 1862 the 1835 church housed wounded. Guns emplaced nearby defended the church against Stonewall Jackson's batteries across the Potomac.

Hyattstown

Generals Stonewall Jackson and Nathaniel P. Banks engaged in an artillery skirmish at the town in 1862.

Kingston

Kingston Hall. At the once elegant estate lived Anna Ella Carroll, daughter of a governor of Maryland (1830-31). She grew up amid her father's many slaves, an experience which later inspired her to free her slaves and become an abolitionist. An anti-Southern political tract Carroll wrote came to the attention of Lincoln, who asked for her opinions about the conduct of the War. After visiting the Mississippi River she outlined a strategy for capturing the waterway. The Union army and navy in part adopted her plan.

La Plata

Port Tobacco. The museum at the site, one of the oldest continuously inhabited English settlements in North America

(1638), includes displays on the War and on John Wilkes Booth. Lincoln conspirator George Atzerodt lived in the area. Smugglers used the port during the War.

Middletown

Battle of South Mountain. The battle took place near Middletown on September 14, 1862, when Lee encountered McClellan during the Confederate general's first invasion of Maryland. The battle, which began at Fox's Gap, a mile south, and continued from there to South Mountain, forced the outflanked Confederates back toward Sharpsburg. Among the some 1800 men on each side killed, wounded or missing was the wounded Colonel Rutherford B. Hayes, future president. (See also the entry for Gathland State Park.)

Nancy Crouse. The seventeen-year-old Middletown resident, who lived on Main Street, supposedly had a Union flag wrapped around her as she watched Confederate cavalrymen riding through town. The passing Rebels ripped the flag away from the defiant Crouse and destroyed it.

Pikesville

Confederate Soldiers Home. The early nineteenth century U.S. Arsenal was occupied by veterans of the War and later wars. The county took over the buildings in 1932.

Point Lookout State Park

Union Prison. Two monuments memorialize the 3384 prisoners of war who died at the Point Lookout Prison Camp during the War. A War museum recalls the era. Inmates built Fort Lincoln at the site, which was one of two forts constructed to defend the mouth of the Potomac and Chesapeake Bay.

Poolesville

White's Ferry. The Potomac River's only ferry boat, near

Poolesville, bears the name *Jubal Early*, recalling the Confederate general's forays in the area. His troops crossed the Potomac here in July 1864 during a retreat from Washington. In September 1862 Lee crossed at this point on his way to Frederick and Antietam, while a month later Jeb Stuart crossed after his raid on Chambersburg, PA. Poolesville changed hands various times during the War.

Queen Anne

Frederick Douglass Birthplace. On highway 328 just west of the Tuckahoe River bridge stands a marker noting the birthplace of the famous black abolitionist (see the entry for his house in the Washington, D.C., section) at a farm two miles south of Queen Anne by present-day highway 303.

Rockville

Confederate Monument. Opposite the courthouse stands an 1813 monument memorializing Montgomery County soldiers who served the South.

Confederate Raids. Confederate soldiers frequently raided Rockville in search of horses. After Jubal Early's encounter with Union general Lew Wallace at the July 9, 1864, Battle of Monocacy (see Frederick), the Confederate forces passed through Rockville on the way to and from their attempt to invade Washington.

Salisbury

Camp Upton. In November 1861 Union forces established the base, on the present-day site of the *Salisbury Times*, to control the eastern shore.

Salisbury and the surrounding area were sharply split during the War, with the many slave owners in the region clashing with Union supporters. Federal troops occupied the town during the War.

Sharpsburg

Kennedy Farmhouse. In the summer of 1859 John Brown

collected arms and men at the farmhouse in preparation for his October 17 raid on Harpers Ferry.

Snow Hill

Julia A. Purnell Museum. The museum, which covers the history of Worchester County, includes War items.

Sparks

Milton Inn. The 1828 stone stagecoach stop later housed Milton Academy, where John Wilkes Booth was a student.

St. Michaels

Museum of Costume. Displays include pantaloons worn by Mary Todd Lincoln and a vest worn by Clark Gable in the War epic *Gone with the Wind.*

Cannons. Near the harbor stand replicas of two cannons given to the town in 1813. At the beginning of the War Union troops from a Federal arsenal at Easton confiscated the originals.

Victoriana Inn. Union officer Dr. Clay Dodson built the house, now a bed and breakfast establishment, in 1865.

Taneytown

Antrim. The cupola on the front section of the 1844 Greek Revival-style house served as a lookout for Union commander George G. Meade, who used the residence as his headquarters before Gettysburg.

Crouse's Mill. Meade stationed a unit at the mill on Big Pipe Creek to defend against Lee's advance through the area.

Union Mills Homestead

Before the Battle of Gettysburg, both Union and Confederate troops stopped to eat at the Homestead, built in 1797. The mill across the road served as an overnight stop for Jeb Stuart's Confederate cavalry and for Union soldiers.

Vienna

Hicks House. Thomas Holliday Hicks, governor of Maryland at the outbreak of the War when the border state wavered between North and South, called a special session of the General Assembly to consider secession. When Union troops occupied Annapolis the Assembly was directed to convene at Frederick (see that entry). Hicks, who served in the U.S. Senate from 1862 until his death in 1865, is buried in Cambridge.

Waldorf

Dr. Samuel A. Mudd Museum. At the antique-furnished two-story 1830s frame house lived the doctor who treated the leg fracture of John Wilkes Booth. Lincoln's assassin injured the limb in leaping to the stage of Ford's Theatre as he shouted "*Sic semper tyrannis!*" The South is avenged!" Although unaware that Booth had assassinated Lincoln, Dr. Mudd was sentenced to life imprisonment. He was freed after four years (see the Fort Jefferson entry in the Florida section).

Washington Monument State Park

The thirty-four foot stone tower (1827) was the first completed monument to George Washington. The History Center in the park houses War items.

Westminster

The town served as a Union supply depot during the Battle of Gettysburg. As the two armies advanced toward Gettysburg before the battle, a number of encounters occurred in the Westminster area.

Missouri

Arrow Rock

Sappington Cemetery State Historic Site. Graves include that of Claiborne Fox Jackson, the pro-Southern governor of Missouri during the War who tried to swing the border state into the Confederacy.

Athens

Battle of Athens State Historic Site. In the far northeastern corner of Missouri lies the site of the War's most northern encounter west of the Mississippi. Although outnumbered four to one, Union forces managed to repel a Rebel attack on August 5, 1861. The Southern units included two sons of the Union commander. Only a few buildings and a ruined mill recall the nearly vanished town.

Thome-Benning House. The mid-1840s frame residence, known as the Cannonball House, bears at the front and rear walls holes made by a cannonball which passed through the building.

Belmont

At the now extinct settlement of Belmont, which stood on the banks of the Mississippi River opposite Columbus, Kentucky (see that entry), occurred Grant's first direct encounter with Southern forces. In early November 1861 Grant led 3100 men from his base at Cairo, Illinois (see that entry), to attack a Rebel encampment at Belmont. The November 7 skirmish, which ended indecisively, might be considered the beginning of the long battle to control the Mississippi. In his *Personal Memoirs* Grant recalled that when Southern soldiers sighted him their commander said, "There is a Yankee; you may try your marksmanship on him if you wish." For some reason, the men withheld their fire, so sparing Grant for the great campaign he later led.

Bennett Spring State Park

The spring and the park are named for mill owner Peter Bennett, who during the War donated grain and flour to impoverished families.

Boonville

On June 17, 1861, Union troops, under General Nathaniel Lyon (see that entry in the St. Louis section) defeated state militia commanded by Colonel John S. Marmaduke. The victory ensured Union control of the Missouri River in this area. The Battle of Boonville was the first battle of the War in Missouri and one of the first anywhere. A second encounter took place in Boonville in the fall of 1863.

Butler

Butler County Museum of Pioneer History. The museum includes War items.

Order No. 11. On August 25, 1863, General Thomas Ewing issued the later famous Order No. 11, which mandated evacuation of many areas in western Missouri to prevent residents from aiding guerrilla raiders in the region. After issuance of the order, the town of Butler was burned.

Canton

Culver-Stockton College. The Union used the campus as a headquarters.

Cape Girardeau

Fort D. Earthworks and rifle pits of Fort D, largest of the Union's four forts in Cape Girardeau, survive. According to legend, soldiers at the fort, located near the Mississippi, used cannonballs to bowl on the town green. Historical markers recall the April 26, 1863, encounter when Confederate forces suffered heavy losses.

Court of Common Pleas. The basement of the 1854 courthouse, perched atop a steep hill overlooking downtown, served as a prison to hold captured Confederates.

Port Cape Girardeau. The riverfront restaurant occupies an 1830s building used by Grant as a headquarters.

Carthage

Jasper County Museum. Installed in the imposing 1895 county courthouse, built of the local marble, the museum includes War uniforms, guns and swords.

Battle of Carthage. On July 5, 1861, the state's second major War encounter took place near Carthage when the Missouri State Guard, commanded by Governor Claiborne Jackson, defeated Federal troops. The town changed hands several times during the War. Southern guerrillas finally destroyed Carthage in 1864, setting fire to the town, which burned to the ground.

Carver National Monument

The George Washington Carver National Monument includes the farm where the future famous scientist was born in the early 1860s to a slave woman named Mary. Confederate guerrillas raided the farm and kidnapped the boy and his mother, who disappeared. Carver, however, was found in Arkansas and returned to the farm, where he lived as a child. A trail takes visitors to the birthplace site, a statue of Carver, and the family cemetery.

Cassville

In early November 1861 Southern sympathizers in the Missouri legislature met in Cassville and passed an ordinance of secession, but it never took effect.

Centralia

William "Bloody Bill" Anderson. Historical markers recall the September 1864 raid led by Anderson, whose band of guerrillas, including Frank and Jesse James, looted the town and killed twenty-five Union soldiers after stopping the train they were on. Anderson (see the entry for him under Richmond), killed a month later by a Union officer, spread terror in western Missouri and eastern Kansas as part of the 150 or so Confederate sympathizing renegades led by William C. Quantrill (see Higginsville), head of the War's most famous guerrilla band.

Fulton

Battle of Moore's Mill. A diorama at the Callaway County courthouse depicts the July 28, 1862, encounter, its site marked by a plaque on highway JJ.

"The Kingdom of Callaway." Callaway County became known as "The Kingdom of Callaway" during the War. The name originated in October 1861 when local Confederate sympathizers, defending the area with logs designed to resemble cannons, negotiated a treaty with a Union officer, so elevating the county—at least in the eyes of its residents—to a sovereign power equal in status to the U.S.

Greenfield

Greenfield Museum. Two rooms at the museum, installed in the old 1870 Washington Hotel, contain items from the War and the two World Wars.

Hulston Mill. Located seven miles east of Greenfield, the mill supplied grain to troops in the Springfield area. Home guards patrolled the mill to protect it from destruction by marauding Confederate guerrillas.

Higginsville

State Confederate Home. On the grounds of the Home, razed after the last occupant died in 1950 at age 108, survive a few original buildings, including the hospital and the chapel.

Confederate Memorial State Historic Site. The cemetery at the site includes the graves of 603 Southern veterans and 225 wives. In

October 1992 the meager remains—five bones and a vial of hair—of William Clark Quantrill were interred at the Confederate Cemetery. Quantrill, a notorious War era guerrilla, led some 350 Southern sympathizers on the devastating August 21, 1863, raid at Lawrence, Kansas. After being killed by Federal troops on May 10, 1865, Quantrill was buried in an unmarked grave in Louisville. The Kansas Historical Society later obtained five of his bones, which in 1992 were laid to rest at the cemetery in Higginsville.

Ironton

Fort Davidson State Historic Site. Well preserved earthworks and a well presented museum recall the fort and the September 27, 1864, Battle of Pilot Knob, which occurred when Confederate general Sterling Price attacked the installation in his drive north to capture St. Louis. Under cover of night, Union general Thomas Ewing led his men to a safe escape. From here, Price turned west and engaged Union forces at Jefferson City, Boonville, Glasgow and Lexington before his defeat at Westport (see that entry under Kansas City) on October 23, 1864, so ending the Confederate threat to Missouri.

Courthouse. The eastern and southern walls of the 1858 building bear damage from cannon fire. During the War the courthouse served as a hospital and barracks.

Grant Monument. The striking statue stands on the spot where, as the inscription notes, Colonel Grant "received his commission as general, 1861, and parting from his rest entered on his career of victory."

Jefferson City

State Capitol. After Governor Clairborne Fox Jackson refused to accept the pro-Union vote of a special convention, Federal troops took possession of the city and camped on capitol hill. In his March westward across Missouri in 1864, Confederate general Sterling Price threatened the state capital but failed to take it.

Displays at the Missouri State Museum in the capitol include weapons, unit battle flags and other War items.

Lincoln University. Black War soldiers raised $6000 to establish the school in 1866 as an institute to train black teachers. It became a state university in 1921.

Parsons House. The 1830s residence, used by both sides as a hospital, belonged to Monroe Mosby Parsons, a Confederate general who refused to surrender at the end of the War. Parsons, who organized the Missouri State Militia and fought under Price, went to Mexico to join nationalistic forces fighting Maximilian and was killed there on August 17, 1865.

G.H. Dulle. The 1857 residence served as Union headquarters.

National Cemetery. Union soldiers repose at the burial ground, while at the adjacent Woodlawn Cemetery lies Confederate general John S. Marmaduke.

Kansas City

Westport. Twenty-five numbered markers trace the course of the Battle of Westport, the largest encounter west of the Mississippi. On October 23, 1864, about 9000 Confederate troops clashed with some 20,000 Union soldiers, who forced Sterling Price's forces to retreat, so ending the Confederate threat to Missouri.

Union Cemetery. So named not for the Union but because it served both Kansas City and Westport, the burial ground, established in 1857, includes fifteen Confederate graves, marked by a ten foot granite monument. Also buried there is artist George Caleb Bingham, whose famous painting of General Thomas Ewing's unpopular Order No. 11 (see the Butler entry) influenced public opinion against Ewing, who hoped for a political career after the War. The painting is owned by the State Historical Society on the campus of the University of Missouri in Columbia.

The Black Archives of Mid-America. The museum and library includes items relating to black participants in the War.

Independence. The Kansas City suburb was twice captured for one day by Confederate forces. Five markers in the area recount the story of the October 1864 Battle of Independence. Confederate guerrillas Frank James and William Quantrill were imprisoned during the War at the Jackson County Jail, now a museum.

Kearney

James Brothers. War guerrillas—and, later, famed and feared bank robbers—Jesse and Frank James were born at the James Farm, now open to the public. Jesse is buried at Mount Olivet cemetery in Kearney. Frank James reposes in the Hill Family Cemetery in Independence.

Kennett

Dunklin County Museum. The museum houses the "Birthright Letters," a collection of correspondence between former slaves and their owners. After passing a resolution to secede from the Union, the southern Missouri county became known as the Independent State of Dunklin.

Keytesville

General Sterling Price Museum. The museum bears the name of the Confederate general who struggled to capture Missouri for the South, a campaign which ended with his defeat at Westport (see that entry under Kansas City and see the Fort Davidson entry under Ironton). A statue of Price stands in the city park at Keytesville, home town of the later renowned general, Joint Chiefs of Staff Chairman Maxwell D. Taylor.

Lee's Summit

Cole Younger Grave. At the cemetery reposes the notorious War era guerrilla (died 1916), who rode with Quantrill's Raiders.

Lexington

Battle of Lexington State Historic Site. From September 12-20, 1861, 3500 Union soldiers defended the town against 12,000 attackers. Advancing behind protective bales of hemp, the Southerners overwhelmed the Union forces to win the "Battle of the Hemp Bales," as the encounter came to be called.

Anderson House. The 1853 house, which served as a hospital, is now a museum housing War items which recall the local battle.

Lafayette County Courthouse. Price occupied the 1849 building as his headquarters. A cannonball still embedded at the top of the far left column survives as a relic of the Union shelling.

Union Headquarters. Colonel James Mulligan occupied the old Masonic College as his headquarters. In Central College Park stands a one-quarter size replica of the original building, completed in 1848.

Lexington Historical Museum. The museum, installed in the 1846 Cumberland Presbyterian Church, includes a diorama of the local battle and War artifacts.

Liberty

William Jewell College. In 1861 Federal troops used The Hall, a c. 1850 classic revival building, as a hospital and stable.

Lone Jack

Civil War Museum of Jackson County. A small round building at the site of the August 16, 1862, Battle of Lone Jack houses displays and four dioramas relating to the encounter, which resulted in a retreat by Federal troops.

Maramec Spring Park

Maramec Iron Works. Part of the 1857 cold-blast furnace survives at the iron works, established in 1826. During the War the firm supplied iron for cannonballs and gunboats.

Memphis

Downing Mansion. Union soldiers occupied the National Register-listed house, distinctive for its three story Italianate-type tower. As evidenced by horseshoe marks on the original pine floor (now covered by oak flooring), the troops rode horses into the house.

Meramec Caverns

During the War gunpowder was manufactured for the Union army at the caverns, located near Stanton off Interstate 44. In 1864 guerrilla raider William Quantrill, whose band included Frank and Jesse James, captured the gunpowder operation at the cave.

Mexico

Ross House. Colonel Ulysses S. Grant was supposedly at the 1857 house when he learned by reading a newspaper article of his promotion to brigadier general. The residence, listed on the National Register, houses the county historical museum, while on the grounds of the estate is the American Saddle Horse Museum.

Mount Vernon

Lawrence County Museum. Displays include a number of War items.

Nevada

Bushwacker Museum. The name of the museum—which occupies the former jail, in use from 1860 to 1960—refers to the name given to Confederate guerrillas who terrorized western Missouri and eastern Kansas during the War. Displays at the museum include War memorabilia. In May 1863 Bushwackers raided Nevada, ambushing a Northern militia unit.

New Madrid

New Madrid Historical Museum. Displays include uniforms, military equipment, and artifacts from the battle at New Madrid.

Island No. 10. During the early part of the War Southern forces occupied New Madrid. On March 14, 1862, the Union took control of the town, which the Federals used as a base to launch a campaign to capture nearby Island No. 10, a Confederate stronghold from which the Southerners could block Northern boats on the Mississippi. On April 8 General John Pope captured the strategic island, a key victory in the Union drive to gain control of the river.

Ozark

Christian County Museum. The museum occupies the 1880 house of Lucile Adams, the first woman newspaper reporter in the area. Exhibits include War items.

Palmyra

Palmyra Massacre. A marker on the courthouse grounds recounts the story of an episode Lincoln adjudged one of the most despicable of the War. After Confederate Colonel John C. Porter refused to release a captured Northern spy, the Union commander executed ten Confederate captives on October 18, 1862.

Richmond

Ray County Museum. The Civil War Room includes uniforms, weapons and other War artifacts.

"Bloody Bill" Anderson. The War era guerrilla, who participated in Quantrill's August 23, 1863, raid on Lawrence, Kansas, was killed in 1864 and is buried in Richmond at the Old City Cemetery.

Rolla

Phelps County Courthouse. Construction of the building began in 1860 but work ceased during the War. The Union used the partly completed structure as a storehouse for hay and grain to feed cavalry horses and, later, as a hospital.

Forts. Fort Wyman stood atop a hill by present day U.S. highway 63 about a mile south of the courthouse, while Fort Dette, built in 1863, stood at a site now occupied by the Missouri School of Mines.

St. Joseph

Patee House Museum. The former hotel, best known as the office of the Pony Express (founded in St. Joseph in 1860), served as a Union recruiting office. Lincoln's Secretary of State, William Seward, once addressed a hostile crowd from the hotel balcony.

St. Louis

Old Courthouse. Slaves were sold at auction on the Fourth Street steps of the courthouse. The last attempt to sell slaves in St. Louis took place in 1861 when the auction was cancelled after 2000 people demonstrated against the event. Exhibits at the Old Courthouse recount the story of the 1847 Dred Scott trial held there. The slave won his suit for freedom, but the ruling was reversed on appeals to the Missouri and U.S. Supreme Court, when a seven to two ruling against Scott in 1857 was one of the incidents which led to the War. Scott's owner later freed him.

Cemeteries. Scott (died 1858) is buried at Calvary Cemetery in north St. Louis, as are Union generals William Tecumseh Sherman and Don Carlos Buell. At nearby Bellefontaine Cemetery repose Sterling Price, the Confederate general who attempted to capture Missouri for the South, and James B. Eads, builder of War boats for the Union.

Carondelet. Eads built seven iron-clad gunboats, used by the Union to gain control of the Mississippi, at his works at the east end of Marceau Street in Carondelet south of St. Louis. A separate city during the War, Carondelet merged with St. Louis in 1871.

Eads also built St. Louis's famous Eads Bridge, dedicated in 1874 by Grant, then president.

Grant's Farm. Owned by the Busch family of Anheuser-Busch brewing fame, the property includes the 1856 cabin built by Grant when he lived here at the farm he called Hardscrabble. Free tours of the estate (by reservation only: 314-843-1700) are offered from mid-April to mid-October.

Jefferson Barracks. Lieutenant U.S. Grant, an 1843 West Point graduate, was stationed at Jefferson Barracks, established in 1826, when he married St. Louisian Julia Dent. A few 1850s stone buildings survive at Jefferson Barracks Park, where many War military greats served before the conflict. These included Union generals Sherman, Buell and John C. Fremont, and Confederate generals Joseph E. Johnston and John Bell Hood. Jefferson Davis arrived at the fort in 1828, and in 1855 Lee, then a colonel, served as commanding officer at the post. During the War a hospital was built at Jefferson Barracks, whose wharfs and docking facilities served the newly organized hospital ship fleet of the Union navy. In 1863 the Jefferson Barracks National Cemetery, one of eight such cemeteries established then, was opened. The burial ground includes the graves of 12,000 Union men and more than 1000 Confederates. Only in 1906 did Federal authorities authorize marking the graves of the Southern dead.

White Haven. In the 1850s the Grants lived at White Haven, a 1000 acre plantation. In 1990 the National Park Service acquired ten acres and the original house, now undergoing restoration and eventually to open as a National Historic Site.

Captain Nathaniel Lyon Statue. The monument stands in Lyon Park at Arsenal Street and South Broadway across from the Anheuser-Busch brewery. Lyon commanded the Federal Arsenal, which housed the largest store of munitions in the West. Lyon defended the Arsenal, located at the southeast corner of Second and Arsenal Streets not far from the statue, against attempts by Confederates to capture the facility.

Camp Jackson. In May 1861 Lyon's regular troops and a home guard unit, comprised mainly of German immigrants trained by Lyon, occupied Camp Jackson, located near today's Grand Boulevard and Lawton Avenue. Federal forces captured 639 Southern militiamen during the episode. Riots broke out as Lyon's units marched the captives to the Arsenal, resulting in the deaths of four Union and twenty-seven Confederate soldiers, the only War fatalities which occurred in St. Louis. Among the on-lookers was William Tecumseh Sherman, then living in St. Louis, who joined the Union army as a colonel a few days later. Lyon was killed at Wilson's Creek (see that entry) near Springfield, Missouri.

Confederate Monument. Near Confederate Drive in Forest Park—off Lindell, not far east of Jefferson Memorial—stands the 1914 monument, bronze figures showing a recruit leaving to join the Confederate army as three people look anxiously at the departing youth. The inscription observes that Southerners "fought to uphold the right declared by the pen of Jefferson and achieved by the sword of Washington." The controversial monument, the only one in Forest Park which required a city ordinance, provoked one councilman to argue that if the project was not appoved St. Louis's trade with the South might suffer.

Mercantile Library. This membership library downtown houses a treasure trove of books, archives and historical items, some relating to the War.

Springfield

National Cemetery. Some 1500 Union soldiers repose at the cemetery, established in 1867. Next to it opened a Confederate cemetery, where more than 500 Southerners are buried. In 1911 the National Cemetery absorbed the smaller burial ground with the stipulation that only Southern veterans and their families could be buried in the Confederate cemetery. But because the National Cemetery needed more space, in 1983 Congress voted to allow non-Southerners to be interred in the Confederate section.

Tipton

Maclay House. Built in 1858 as a seminary for young ladies, the structure served as a Union headquarters.

Monuments in town mark the graves of two Union infantry men killed during a skirmish.

Warrensburg

Old Johnson County Courthouse. Forces from both sides occupied the building, the state's oldest remaining courthouse (1842). At the beginning of the War Warrensburg, like Missouri, was divided, with the Confederate militia drilling on the west side of town and the Union militia on the east side.

Watkins Mill State Historic Site

Established in 1861, the mill supplied blankets and cloth to both armies. The facility, a National Historic Landmark, is the nation's only surviving fully equipped nineteenth century textile mill.

Wilson's Creek National Battlefield

The park, ten miles southwest of Springfield, was opened on August 10, 1961, one hundred years to the day after one of the War's first major encounters took place at the site. The visitor center houses displays which trace the story of the bloody battle that resulted in some 1300 soldiers on each side killed, wounded or missing. A five mile drive around the park takes visitors to buildings and positions occupied by the combatants. During the encounter Nathaniel Lyon (see the St. Louis listing) became the first Union general to be killed in battle during the War.

Pennsylvania

Allentown

Soldiers' and Sailors' Monument. In Center Square stands a hundred foot granite shaft whose base includes life-size figures of War soldiers.

Altona

Baker Mansion. The mid-1840s residence of ironmaster Elias Baker contains exhibits on Lincoln.

Athens

Tioga Point Museum. The museum, installed in the Spaulding Memorial Building, includes war memorabilia.

Bedford

Bedford Springs Hotel. The hotel, the so called "Summer White House" of James Buchanan, stands four miles south of Bedford. In 1859 President Buchanan announced he would not seek a second term, opening the way for Lincoln's election.

Bloomsburg

Fishing Creek "Confederacy." Late in the War a confederacy of draft evaders supposedly occupied Fishing Creek Valley near Bloomsburg. The Union sent a thousand soldiers into the area, but the soldiers found no evidence of any settlement or confederacy of draft dodgers.

Boalsburg

Pennsylvania Military Museum. The museum, which traces the history of Pennsylvania servicemen from the Revolution through Viet Nam, includes War items.

Caledonia

Caledonia Furnace. Ardent abolitionist Thaddeus Stevens (see Lancaster) established the furnace in 1837 to provide work to the needy. On June 28, 1863, Confederate general Jubal Early made a detour from his direction of advance especially to destroy the property of the out-spoken anti-slavery Northerner.

Carlisle

Dickinson College. In June 1863, Confederate general A.G. Jenkins' force of some 500 cavalry, energized by their victory at Chambersburg, invaded the town. The first wave of invaders was followed by General Richard S. Ewell's units, some of whose men camped on the college grounds. Confederate forces occupied Carlisle for three days. Union soldiers entered the town as the retreating Southerners shelled it. Graduates of the college include James Buchanan, Lincoln's immediate predecessor, and Roger B. Taney, U.S. Supreme Court chief justice during the War (see Taney House in the Frederick, Maryland, entry).

Chambersburg

Confederate forces occupied the town three times. During the last occupation on July 30, 1864, they burned the city when it refused to pay an indemnity of $100,000 in gold. Chambersburg thus became the only Northern town burned by the Confederates during the War.

John Brown. Brown established his headquarters at 225 King Street prior to his raid on Harpers Ferry.

Chamberfest. Chambersburg celebrates its War history with the annual Chamberfest festival in late July.

Clark

Tara. The 1845 country inn, which houses three restaurants, takes its name from the famous mansion in the War epic *Gone with* *the Wind.* Guides in War era costumes conduct tours through the rooms, filled with antiques and period furnishings.

Easton

Soldiers' and Sailors' Monument. The 1899 monument honors Northampton County's War veterans.

Gettysburg

Gettysburg National Military Park. The 3500 acre park includes more than 1300 monuments, statues and markers, many of them along the thirty-one miles of marked roads. The visitor center houses War artifacts and an electronic map highlighting the July 1-3, 1863, battle, the bloodiest of the conflict, with 51,000 casualties. Across from the visitor center lies the National Cemetery, with 3706 War dead and the Soldiers' National Monument, located near where Lincoln delivered his address on November 19, 1863. The Cyclorama Center houses the "Pickett's Charge" painting, centerpiece of a sound and light show. The park also includes a number of other features which recall the famous battle. Gettysburg is the only national battlefield with guides licensed by the federal government. Some one hundred official guides are available to take visitors on a two hour driving tour of the park. Guide service can be arranged at the visitor center.

"The Conflict." Multi-image productions trace the history of the War. "Three Days at Gettysburg" covers the local battle, while "The War Within" deals with the entire War. A one-man show entitled "A. Lincoln's Place" dramatizes the famous man's life and career from log house to White House.

Lincoln Room Museum. The Wills House, where the president stayed in 1863 and where he completed the Address, includes original furnishings.

Lee's Headquarters and Museum. Displays at the eighteenth century house, the Southern general's headquarters, include military items, War photos and documents.

National Tower. The 307-foot observation tower affords views of the Military Park. An audio program describes the battle which unfolded below.

Gettysburg Battle Theatre. A half hour multi-media program explains the encounter by using a miniature battlefield with 25,000 figures.

National Civil War Wax Museum. More than 200 wax figures and an audiovisual presentation evoke the War and the battle.

Gettysburg College. Pennsylvania Hall served as a hospital during the War. The college's Lincoln and Soldiers Institute offers a prize for excellence in War studies.

Grand Army of the Republic Highway

The GAR Highway, U.S. 6—which extends from Provincetown, Massachusetts, to Bishop, California—was named to honor Union War veterans. In 1937 the Sons of the Union Veterans of the Civil War suggested that U.S. 6, then the second longest federal route (3652 miles), be declared a memorial highway. "Grand Army of the Republic" signs designate the route along its length. On the highway in Pennsylvania, where the road runs along the state's northern edge, lies the town of Kane (see entry), founded by a Union general.

Hanover

Hanover Battle. On June 30, 1863, the first battle north of the Mason-Dixon line took place at Hanover when Union generals Hugh Kilpatrick and George Custer (later of Indian wars fame) defeated forces led by Jeb Stuart, thus preventing the Confederate general from reaching Gettysburg until a day after the main encounter there.

Harrisburg

State Museum of Pennsylvania. The museum's Military Gallery is devoted mainly to the War. One of the world's largest framed paintings depicts Pickett's charge at Gettysburg, while cannons flanking the painting punctuate the scene. Displays honor five Pennsylvania companies known as the "First Defenders" because the units were the first Northern volunteers to reach Washington in April 1861 after Lincoln's call for volunteers.

Camp Curtin. The first Union concentration camp, named for the governor, was established in Harrisburg.

In the summer of 1863 a unit of Lee's army reached the edge of Harrisburg, but then decided not to proceed to invade the Susquehanna Valley.

Fort Washington. At the corner of 8th and Ohio Streets in Lemoyne, a suburb of Harrisburg, stood Fort Washington, the northernmost point of Confederate invasion during the War. On June 29, 1863, Confederate cavalry, reconnoitering the southwestern approach to the state capital, exchanged volleys with Union troops defending the area. Tensions ran high in the Harrisburg area as the two armies massed at nearby Gettysburg prepared to clash in fateful battle.

Honesdale

Wayne County Historical Society Museum. Displays include War memorabilia and the diary of Reverend Dr. Kidder, an honorary pallbearer for Lincoln.

Kane

Thomas L. Kane. Located on the Grand Army of the Republic Highway, the town was founded by Union general Thomas L. Kane, Pennsylvania's first volunteer in the War. The Kane Memorial Chapel and a museum honor the general. Grant was once arrested in Kane for fishing without a license.

Lancaster

Wheatland. At the 1828 house—described as a "beau ideal of a statesman's abode"—lived James Buchanan, who conducted his

1856 presidential campaign from the library at Wheatland. Buchanan served as president in the years leading up to the War (1857-1861).

Thaddeus Stevens. At Shreiner's Cemetery reposes the War era U.S. representative from Pennsylvania, one of the nations's leading figures in the fight to eliminate slavery. From 1843 until his death in 1868 Stevens lived in Lancaster at 45 South Queen Street. At the abolitionist's funeral, five of his pallbearers were black. Stevens specified burial in the only Lancaster cemetery which allowed black interments in order "that I might illustrate in my death the principles which I advocated through a long life."

Lewisburg

Slifer House Museum. The twenty room mansion was the residence of Eli Slifer, secretary of the Commonwealth of Pennsylvania during the War. Displays on the second floor include historic memorabilia.

Ligonier

Forbes Road Gun Museum. Displays include War firearms.

Meadville

Allegheny College. The library houses a collection of Lincoln material.

Mercersburg

Buchanan Birthplace. On the campus of Mercersburg Academy stands the log cabin where James Buchanan, Lincoln's immediate predecessor, was born in 1791. The cabin originally stood near Cove Gap on highway 16 in what is now the James Buchanan State Forest.

Underground Railroad. Mercersburg's location near the Mason-Dixon line and narrow passes through nearby mountains made the town an ideal stop on the Underground Railroad. Twenty-five families of fugitive slaves opted not to flee farther north, instead establishing in the area a settlement they called Africa.

Mont Alto

Episcopal Chapel. John Brown taught Sunday school at the sanctuary, located on Penn State's Mont Alto campus, while he prepared for his raid on Harpers Ferry.

Philadelphia

Civil War Library and Museum. The library includes some 16,000 War books, while the museum contains rooms designated Confederate, Grant, Navy, Relics and Weapons. A room upstairs devoted to Lincoln houses plaster casts of his hands and face.

Independence Hall. Lincoln was at the Hall both just before and just after his presidency. On February 22, 1861, he spoke as president-elect on the way to his inaugural. During the ceremony Lincoln raised a thirty-four star flag and stated that he would "consider myself one of the happiest men in the world" if he could save the Union. On April 22, 1865, Lincoln's body was brought to the Hall where the president lay in state as more than 85,000 people passed by the bier.

Smith Civil War Memorial. At the entrance to Memorial Hall in Fairmount Park stand columns given in 1890 as a War Memorial by Richard Smith, a foundry owner and printer. Union leaders depicted in bronze include generals George Meade and John Reynolds, while Smith himself is also shown.

Civil War Soldiers and Sailors Memorial. Two marble pylons (installed 1927) at the entrance to the tree-lined section of the Parkway, near the Museum of Art, bear lists of major War battles and naval encounters.

National Archives. The Philadelphia branch of the Archives includes War records.

War Houses. Grant occupied a house at 20th and Chestnut

Streets, and Meade, the Union commander at Gettysburg, lived at 19th and Delancey Streets.

Mother Bethel African Methodist Church The 1890 church, fourth on the site, occupies the oldest piece of land continuously owned by blacks in the U.S. The original church dated from 1787. The War era church served as a stop on the Underground Railroad.

Johnson House. The 1768 residence, at 6306 Germantown Avenue, was a station on the Underground Railroad.

Laurel Hill Cemetery. Confederate general John C. Pemberton is buried here.

Pittsburgh

Soldiers and Sailors Memorial. Dedicated in 1910, the memorial includes a museum which features War memorabilia, among them portraits, personal items, weapons, medical and band instruments, and a tree trunk fragment with two cannonballs embedded in it during the Battle of Chickamauga.

Arsenal. At the northwest corner of Butler and 40th Streets stood Allegheny Arsenal, one of the North's leading depots during the Mexican, Civil and Spanish-American Wars.

Pottsville

Henry Clay Monument. The memorial to the Kentuckian (see Lexington, Kentucky) and three time presidential candidate recalls the Whig politician who tried to keep the United States from disuniting in the years leading up to the War. The ninety foot high monument—built in 1855 and supposedly the nation's oldest cast-iron statue—honors the Southerner for supporting legislation favorable to the region's coal industry.

Reading

The town claims a quartet of War firsts: the first regiment formed, the first War flag, the first volunteer band, the first women's aid society.

Lincoln Homestead. In the environs lived Mordecai Lincoln, the president's great-great-grandfather. He arrived in the area in 1720 and later occupied a brownstone house. Lincoln ancestors (as well as those of frontiersman Daniel Boone) repose at the Exeter Friends Burying Ground in the area.

Scranton

War Monuments. In Courthouse Square stand monuments to General Philip H. Sheridan and to War dead.

Towanda

David Wilmot. At Riverside Cemetery reposes the U.S. senator who introduced the Wilmot Proviso, requiring the U.S. to outlaw slavery in any lands acquired from Mexico.

Washington

Le Moyne House. Abolitionist politician Francis J. LeMoyne lived at the 1812 house, a station on the Underground Railroad and now the Washington County Historical Society. Up to twenty-six escaped slaves could hide in a secret room on the third floor of what seems to be a two story house. LeMoyne (died 1879) reposes at the nearby site of a crematory he built in 1876, said to be the nation's first such facility.

Waynesboro

Abolitionist John Brown taught Sunday school in the town while he planned his raid on Harpers Ferry.

West Chester

At the town in 1842 was published the *Jeffersonian,* one of only a few newspapers in the North which favored the Southern cause. Rioters wrecked the offices of the paper, whose distribution by mail the postmaster banned.

On July 23, 1863, Jubal Early entered the town, demanding not a ransom of dough, as was his practice, but that local housewives use dough to bake bread for his troops.

Washington, D.C.

Brady Studio

At 627 Pennsylvania Avenue stood the four story brick building where Matthew Brady, the famous War photographer, maintained his studio in the upper floors. At the first encounter he photographed, the Battle of Bull Run, Confederates captured Brady's traveling darkroom wagon, camera and supplies, but he replaced the equipment and covered many subsequent War episodes.

Capitol

Old Senate Chamber. Used by the Senate until 1859, and thereafter by the Supreme Court, the room saw many spirited debates on issues leading up to the War. Here, Henry Clay, Daniel Webster, John C. Calhoun and other politicians argued about slavery, states' rights and preservation of the Union.

Rotunda. In 1953, seventy-six years after work on the original frieze began, artist Allyn Cox added three scenes, one entitled "The Civil War." Statues in the rotunda include Grant and Lincoln.

Churches

Luther Place Memorial Church. After the War the Northern and Southern branches of the Baptist church established the sanctuary at 1226 Vermont Avenue, N.W., as a way of healing wounds created by the conflict.

Metropolitan African Methodist Church. The funeral service for abolitionist Frederick Douglass was held in the sanctuary.

Mt. Zion Church. The city's oldest black church, located in Georgetown, served as a stop on the Underground Railroad. Fleeing slaves were supposedly hidden in a burial vault at the nearby Mt. Zion Cemetery.

New York Avenue Presbyterian Church. The Lincoln family occupied a pew in the church. In the Lincoln Parlor is the original handwritten draft of the Emancipation Proclamation.

Washington National Cathedral. Among the 214 stained glass windows, the first of them installed in 1912, are War related ones in the Lee-Jackson Bay, located at the right front of the nave near the south transept.

Confederate Memorial Hall

A Victorian mansion at 1322 Vermont Avenue, N.W., houses a library and displays, including furniture that once belonged to Jefferson Davis and portraits of Lee and Jackson. By advance notice (202-483-5700), groups can arrange dinner in the mansion.

Ford's Theatre

In the basement of the theater where John Wilkes Booth shot the president is a Lincoln Museum. At the Peterson House across the street Lincoln died. Period furniture and blood stained pillow cases at the house evoke the event.

Forts

At the beginning of the War the capital, threatened by the newly established foreign country just across the Potomac, was virtually undefended. Outmoded Fort Washington (see entry in Maryland section), twelve miles down the Potomac opposite Mount Vernon, was the only installation guarding the city in 1861. By the end of the War, however, a ring of sixty-eight forts and 837 guns surrounded the city to guard its approaches. The National Park Service maintains some of the outposts, collectively known as the Fort Circle Parks, and has partially restored a few. (See entry for Fort Ward at Alexandria, Virginia.)

Fort Stevens Park. Fort Stevens, near present day Georgia

Avenue and Somerset Place, N.W., was the only fort which saw fighting. Now partially restored, the outpost came under fire on July 11 and 12, 1864, as Confederate forces led by Jubal Early were blocked from entering the capital. Lincoln observed the fighting by peering over a parapet at the fort.

Fort Dupont Park. Earthworks atop a ridge survive from the six-sided War fort for which the park was named.

Fort De Russy. In Rock Creek Park, at Oregon and Military Roads, stood the fort to which Lincoln was brought for safety when officials feared a Confederate invasion of the capital.

Fort Leslie J. McNair. At the nation's oldest active military post stood a prison where, on July 7, 1865, four conspirators in Lincoln's assassination were hanged. John Wilkes Booth's body was secretly buried there until 1867; he now reposes in an unmarked grave in Green Mount Cemetery (see that entry) in Baltimore.

Hawn 'n' Dove

Walls at the pub-restaurant, which occupies a War era building, are decorated with Union and Confederate currency.

Houses

Blair-Lee. At the 1824 house a Lincoln emissary offered command of the Union armies to Lee just after the War began. Lee pondered the offer at his mansion (see Arlington, Virginia) and opted for the Confederacy.

Douglass. Famous abolitionist Frederick Douglass, an escaped slave, became the major black figure in the North as the nation moved toward war. He published the *North Star* newspaper, issued his autobiography in 1845, and spoke and wrote on behalf of the black cause all through the 1850s. In 1877 Douglass moved to twenty room Cedar Hill, since 1962 managed by the National Park Service and now restored as it was during Douglass's eighteen year residence there. His first residence in Washington was at 316 A Street, N.E.

Laird-Dunlop. Robert Todd Lincoln, the president's oldest son, lived from 1915 until his death in 1926 in the house at 3014 N Street, N.W., in Georgetown.

Rathbone. At 712 Jackson Place lived Major Henry Rathbone, who accompanied Lincoln to Ford's Theatre and was stabbed by Booth as the assassin tried to escape.

Scott-Grant. Grant spent the summer following the War at the 1858 residence, at 3238 R Street.

Surratt. At the one-time rooming house at 604 H Street, N.W., Booth met with his co-conspirators to plot Lincoln's assassination. The building now houses a shop and private quarters.

Howard University

The traditionally black school, incorporated in 1867, was established as a school for freedmen and named for General Oliver Otis Howard, commissioner of the Freedmen's Bureau. He lived at 1867 Howard Hall, now used as a university office.

Monuments and Memorials

Dupont Circle. The Circle was named in 1882 to honor Admiral Samuel Francis duPont, who in November 1861 sailed his seventeen ships past two Confederate forts to capture Port Royal Sound, South Carolina. The Union navy then installed a base at Port Royal. The present marble fountain replaced the bronze statue of duPont which stood in the circle until 1921.

Farragut Square. The ten foot statue of Admiral David Farragut (see the Fort Morgan, Alabama, entry) was cast from the bronze propeller of his ship, the U.S.S. *Hartford.*

Grand Army of the Republic. The memorial at Pennsylvania Avenue and 7th Street honors Union soldiers.

Grant Memorial. A 250-foot-long sculpture group at the eastern end of the Mall depicts cavalry and artillery units in battle as Grant serenely observes the action.

Lincoln Memorial. On the wall of the landmark is engraved the text of the Gettysburg Address.

Lincoln Statue. At the Department of Interior stands a statue of young Lincoln.

Logan Circle. The 1901 bronze equestrian statue depicts Union General John A. Logan.

McClellan Monument. An image of General George B. McClellan perches atop a horse at Connecticut Avenue and Columbia Road, N.W.

McPherson Square. The bronze equestrian statue of General James B. McPherson, killed during the Battle of Atlanta, was cast from a cannon captured there.

Pike Monument. At 3rd and D Streets, N.W., stands the city's only monument to a Confederate general, Albert Pike.

Sheridan Monument. The statue of General Philip Sheridan, at Massachusetts Avenue and 23rd Street, N.W., is by Gutzon Borglum, who sculpted the presidential faces at Mount Rushmore.

Sherman Monument. The statue on 15th Street stands on the spot where the Union general stood on May 24, 1865, as his victorious army passed in review. More than 200,000 soldiers marched by, perhaps the greatest military parade in U.S. history. Eight bas-reliefs, along with inscriptions and statues, depict Sherman's military career and recount War episodes.

Thomas Circle. The 1879 statue honors General George H. Thomas, called the "Rock of Chickamauga" for his heroic performance at that battle in Georgia.

Museums

In addition to the vast collections at the Smithsonian and at the Library of Congress, the following museums offer more focused War displays.

Armed Forces Medical Museum. Exhibits include material on treatment of the wounded during the War. One item shown is General Daniel Sickle's right leg bone, sent to the museum by him after the limb was amputated during the Battle of Gettysburg. Bone fragments from Lincoln's skull are displayed next to the lead ball Booth fired into the president's head.

Jewish War Veterans National Museum. War items include a gold mezzuzah found at the Chickamauga battlefield, and references to Leopold Karpeles, a Union sergeant who was the first Jew to win the Medal of Honor.

National Building Museum. The world's tallest Corinthian columns, seventy-five feet high, dominate the structure, completed in 1885 as a memorial to War veterans and used over the next forty years to house the Pension Bureau where 1500 employees worked to issue checks to the veterans. Between the first and second floors is a three-foot-high, 1200-foot-long frieze, the nation's largest sculptured terra cotta work, depicting 1355 figures representing units of the Union army.

National Firearms Museum. The museum, which occupies space at the National Rifle Association headquarters, includes War era weapons.

National Museum of American History. Extensive displays on the nation's past include references to the War.

National Museum of Health and Medicine. Established more than 125 years ago, the museum at Walter Reed Army Medical Center includes displays relating to Lincoln's assassination.

Navy Museum. Exhibits cover the role of the navy during the War. On display is the original half model of the *Monitor*, the Union's first iron-clad vessel.

Old Soldiers' Home

Lincoln occasionally spent nights at the 1852 facility, 3700 North Capitol Street, N.W., when the stench from the garbage filled Washington Canal near the White House drove him from the mansion during the summer.

Renwick Gallery

Now part of the Smithsonian, the gallery was originally established in 1861 by banker W.W. Corcoran. The army took over the building to use as a quartermaster's facility. The last year of the War the structure housed the office of Quartermaster General Montgomery C. Meigs, who was instrumental in converting Lee's Arlington, Virginia, estate into a national cemetery after the conflict ended.

Smithsonian

In the lecture hall of the so called "castle," the 1849 Gothic Revival-style building on the Mall, abolitionist newspaper editor Horace Greeley challenged Lincoln in January 3, 1862, to free the slaves, nine months before the president issued the Emancipation Proclamation.

Sumner School

The Charles Sumner School, built in 1872 to educate black children, takes its name from the abolitionist Massachusetts senator, caned by a Congressman in 1856 for delivering an impassioned speech against slavery. The incident inflamed passions on both sides and was a milestone on the road to War. (See the Brooks House entry in Edgefield, South Carolina).

Treasury Building

Built between 1836 and 1869, the building served the Union army as a barracks. For two months after Lincoln's assassination his successor, Andrew Johnson, made his office in the Treasury, where in 1869 Grant held his inaugural ball.

Willard Hotel

The old Willard, on the same corner as the present day establishment, was a gathering place for Union sympathizers. Lincoln

and Grant stayed at the hotel, where in November 1861 Julia Ward
Howe wrote the words to "The Battle Hymn of the Republic."

West Virginia

Ansted

Westlake Cemetery. At the burial ground, on a knoll overlooking the town, is the grave of Julia Neal Jackson, mother of Stonewall Jackson. After Jackson, then a major, visited the grave in 1855,
he wrote an aunt that the site was unmarked. After the War Captain
Thomas D. Ranson, a veteran of the Stonewall Brigade, erected the
marble marker.

Bartow

The village was named for General F.S. Bartow, a Confederate
officer killed at the First Battle of Bull Run. A marker recalls the
December 1861 skirmish at Bartow.

Berkeley Springs

Strother House. General David Hunter Strother bought the
1850 brick residence in 1861. Strother alienated his family by
opting to join the Union army. During the War Northern troops
occupied the house.

Fairfax Inn. The inn, which burned in 1902, occupied a site on
Fairfax Street. The widow who operated the establishment during
the War used her wiles to gather from the resident Union army
colonel information which she passed on to the Confederates.

George Washington and his family often visited Berkeley
Springs, the nation's oldest spa, to take the waters. The War ruined
the resort's business, but it later recovered.

Beverly

Rich Mountain. A marker in the Tygarts Valley town recalls the

Battle of the Rich Mountain, which took place five miles west of there on July 11, 1861. Union general Rosecrans routed the Southern forces, and the Rebels retreated to Laurel Hill (see entry).

Charles Town

Cultural Center. The center, located adjacent to the state capitol, houses the State Museum, with displays on John Brown and on the War. On the capitol grounds stands a monument to Union soldiers and a statue of Stonewall Jackson.

Jefferson County Museum. Featured are John Brown displays and War memorabilia, including the wagon which carried Brown to his execution.

Jefferson County Courthouse. Brown (see Harpers Ferry) was tried in a first floor room of the 1836 building. Even Lincoln, who sympathized with Brown's anti-slavery views, did not object to the agitator's conviction, for we "cannot excuse violence, bloodshed and treason. It could avail him nothing that he might think himself right." The courthouse was shelled during the War.

Old Jail. A latter day building occupies the corner of South George and West Washington Streets where the jail which held Brown stood from about 1803 to 1922.

Brown Gallows. A stone pyramid marks the site where Brown was hanged. Among the 1500 troops guarding the scaffold was a Virginia militiaman named John Wilkes Booth.

Zion Episcopal Church. The churchyard cemetery includes Confederate graves.

Jackson Birth House. At 328 West Main Street stood the small brick house where Stonewall Jackson was born on January 21, 1824. In 1830 he went to live on his grandfather's farm (see Jackson's Mill).

Jackson Cemetery. In the Jackson family plot repose the general's great grandparents, his father and his sister. Also buried there are the sister and mother of Dolley Madison, James Madison's wife.

Lowndes Hill Park. Evidences of Union trenches remain atop the steep hill, given to the city for a park in 1930.

Contentment

The 1830 mansion, on highway 60 seven miles east of Gauley Bridge, belonged to Confederate colonel George W. Imboden. The Fayette County Museum at the site includes War items.

Droop

Droop Mountain Battlefield. The state's largest War battle took place in the area on November 6, 1863, with Union forces defeating the Confederates and ending their last major resistance in West Virginia. A small museum houses War relics, while markers, graves and breastworks in the park recall the encounter.

Elkwater

John Washington. A granite monument commemorates Colonel John Augustine Washington, George Washington's grandnephew. The colonel, who served as Lee's aide-de-camp, was shot from his horse and killed here on September 13, 1861.

Fairmont

Governor Francis H. Pierpont. Pierpont, known as the "father of West Virginia," opposed secession from the Union but favored secession from Virginia. Pierpont attended the Wheeling Conventions, at which the formation of the new state of West Virginia was discussed. At the second Convention Pierpont was elected governor of the "Restored Government of Virginia." At the northeast corner of Pierpont Avenue and Quincy Street stood his house, razed in 1934. Confederates raiding the city on April 29, 1863, burned Pierpont's law library, papers and some of his possessions. Pierpont, who died in 1899, is buried at Woodlawn Cemetery in Fairmont.

During the Confederate raid, General William Ezra Jones's

cavalry division took 260 prisoners and destroyed the railroad bridge across the Monongahela River.

Falling Waters

The Battle of Falling Waters. The encounter took place in July 1863 when Union general George G. Meade attacked Lee's army as it retreated from Gettysburg. Since the bridge over the Potomac had been destroyed by Union soldiers, Lee ordered his men to tear down warehouses along the Chesapeake and Ohio Canal and use the lumber for pontoon bridges. Lee crossed the river by night, and when Meade attacked on July 14 he found that the enemy had fled. A marker notes where Confederate general J.J. Pettigrew died, while another sign indicates where Stonewall Jackson sat under an oak tree when a Union cannonball severed a limb.

Fayetteville

A marker notes the May 19, 1863, episode when Confederates shelled Union fortifications.

Fort Milroy

The Union fort was on 4006-foot White Top Mountain, above the Cheat River near Durbin.

Gauley Bridge

Old Bridge. Stone piers of the bridge destroyed in 1861 by retreating Confederate forces remain.

The town of Gauley Bridge lies in a narrow valley at the confluence of the New and the Gauley Rivers, which form the Great Kanawha. The town's strategic location as the gateway to the valley attracted the attention of both armies. In November 1861 Rosecrans defeated Confederate general John B. Floyd in the last of the battles over control of the valley.

Miller Tavern. The two story frame tavern in town served as a headquarters for Union officers, two of whom became presidents: William McKinley and Rutherford B. Hayes.

Grafton

National Cemetery. More than 2000 soldiers from both armies repose in the burial ground.

Supposedly named for the "graftin' on" of branch rail lines to the main line here, the strategic railroad junction was occupied by both sides. In June 1861 Union general Thomas A. Morris camped in Grafton with 4000 troops before proceeding to Philippi (see entry); later that year McClellan established his headquarters here.

Grantsville

Laid out in 1866, the town was named for Ulysses S. Grant. In the area is Burning Springs, site of oil wells developed in 1860. In 1863 Confederate general William Jones destroyed the wells and set fire to oil-laden barges, sent blazing down the Little Kanawha River.

Halltown

Beall Air. At the estate, about a mile from Halltown, lived Colonel Lewis Washington, great-grandnephew of the president. John Brown kidnapped the colonel on October 16, 1859, the night of the raid on nearby Harpers Ferry. Brown demanded that his captive hand over a sword presented by Frederick the Great of Prussia to George Washington with the compliment, "The oldest general in the world to the greatest." When Brown was captured, he was wearing the heirloom.

Harpers Ferry

In 1790 George Washington himself chose Harpers Ferry, strategically located at the confluence of the Potomac and Shenandoah Rivers, as the site of the National Armory and Arsenal, the target of John Brown's famous raid.

Harpers Ferry National Monument. A visitor center houses displays, while other attractions include period buildings. The Master Armorer's House Museum and the John Brown Museum contain exhibits which recall the raid and its aftermath. The Harpers Ferry Historic Association in town operates a bookstore with a good selection of works on the War.

John Brown Wax Museum. Wax figures and scenes depict the life and death story of Brown, the ardent abolitionist who led a twenty-two man band which raided the National Armory and Arsenal on the night of October 16, 1859. On October 18 the Federal army—officers in the area included Colonel Robert E. Lee and Lieutenant Jeb Stuart—captured the raiders. Brown was tried and on December 2 hung at nearby Charles Town. Six months later, the War broke out. After Virginia seceded in April 1861, Federal troops set fire to the Arsenal but local residents put out the flames and salvaged the weapons, which were sent on to Richmond for use by the Confederate army.

Election Day 1860. This annual pageant includes some one hundred people dressed in period costumes, who re-enact the debates, speeches and demonstrations of the presidential election on the eve of the War. On the ballot in Jefferson County (then Virginia) were Stephen A. Douglas, John C. Breckenridge and John Bell. Voters could not choose Lincoln as he had no elector in the county.

Jackson's Mill

Stonewall Jackson. In 1830, when he was six, Thomas J. (later "Stonewall") Jackson moved from Clarksburg to his grandfather's farm, now the state 4-H Camp. In 1842 he left to attend West Point. Some believe that images of his bucolic days as a lad on the farm inspired Jackson's last words as he lay dying (see Fredericksburg, Virginia): "Let us cross over the river and rest in the shade of the trees."

Keyser

Potomac State College. Part of the school occupies Fort Hill, the site of Fort Fuller, a Federal base attacked in November 1864 by 2000 Confederate troops who seized supplies, burned buildings and destroyed the railroad track. The town, which served as a supply depot for both sides, changed hands fourteen times during the War.

Laurel Hill

Battle of Laurel Hill. At the hill, some seven miles east of Belington, Confederates installed an outpost aimed at blocking McClellan's advance into Virginia. On July 10, 1861, the Union general outflanked the installation and attacked Colonel John Pegram's smaller force on Rich Mountain (see Beverly entry). Confederates at Laurel Hill abandoned the position, and when Rebels fleeing the Rich Mountain rout arrived at Laurel Hill they found that camp empty and were forced to surrender to McClellan, who captured 555 Southerners.

Malden

Booker T. Washington. A marker indicates the site where the future black educator lived with his mother and step-father after leaving Virginia, his birthplace in 1858, following the Emancipation Proclamation.

Martinsburg

Berkeley County Courthouse. Confederate spy Belle Boyd, several times imprisoned in the 1856 courthouse, passed the time by writing in the margins of legal tomes such comments as, "I wonder if I will be shot tomorrow. B. Boyd, April 1863."

Everett House. Both Stonewall Jackson and later Union general Philip Sheridan made their headquarters at the house.

Flick House. To spite the Confederate owner, a Union officer rode his horse through the 1803 residence.

St. John's Lutheran Church. The 1832 sanctuary was remodeled in 1868 to repair damage caused when Union soldiers used the church as a hospital.

Norbourne Hall. At the house lived Union general David Hunter Strother (see Berkeley Springs), who wrote articles under the name "Porte Crayon."

Old Green Hill Cemetery. Graves include these of Strother; Belle Boyd's parents; Ward Hill Lamon, Lincoln's sometime bodyguard during the War; and soldiers from both armies.

Matewan

Hatfield-McCoy. The nearby Tug River Valley was the setting for the Hatfield-McCoy feud, which originated during the War. (See Pike County, Kentucky)

Morgantown

Willey House. Lawyer and politician Waitman T. Willey lived at the residence he built in 1838. Willey, who opposed secession, for a time also opposed West Virginia's secession from Virginia. Willey was elected to the U.S. Senate by the "Restored Government of Virginia," the break-away section of Virginia, and then by the newly created state.

In 1827 one of the Baltimore and Ohio's earliest proposed routes ran through Morgantown, but area residents opposed the new line. Although this proved a mistake in the long run, the absence of a railroad line helped Morgantown avoid the attention of the combatants, and the only War episode here took place in the spring of 1863 when 2000 Confederate troops camped in the town for two days.

Milton

Union Baptist Church. A mile from "Milton-on-the-Mud" (River) stands the 1848 church, occupied by Union troops assigned to protect a nearby covered bridge.

Parkersburg

Nemesis Park. The hilltop park occupies the site of Fort Boreman, built in 1863 by Union forces.

At Parkersburg were held meetings which led to the formation of West Virginia in 1863.

Parsons

Courthouse. On the courthouse lawn stands the Battle of Corrick's Ford Monument. On July 13, 1861, Union forces overtook Confederates retreating from Laurel Hill (see that entry) and defeated the Rebels in an encounter south of town. Confederate general Robert S. Garnett, wounded during the battle, died afterwards in the arms of his West Point classmate, Thomas A. Morris, a Union general.

Philippi

Barbour County Historical Society Museum. The museum, which occupies the restored Baltimore and Ohio station, includes War items.

Alderson-Broaddus College. A marker on the campus of the school, on Broaddus Hill overlooking town, refers to what is described as the "First land battle between the North and the South." On June 3, 1861—three weeks after Fort Sumter—the two sides clashed in an encounter known as the "Philippi Races," so called because of the speed with which Confederate troops retreated when Federal forces attacked at dawn. The Union launched the attack to protect and retain control of the Baltimore and Ohio Railroad, the main line between Washington and the West.

Rainelle

Lee Headquarters. Above the town towers 3170-foot Big Sewell Mountain, where Lee established his headquarters in the fall of 1861. While beneath "Lee's Tree," the Confederate general supposedly received his horse Traveller, originally named Jeff Davis.

All through the War Lee rode the horse, and after the conflict the trusty steed carried its master to Lexington, Virginia, when Lee became president of Washington College there. Traveller died in the 1870s while lying on a feather mattress, and his bones were mounted for display in the Lee Memorial Chapel at Washington and Lee University.

Romney

Keller House. At the corner of Main and Grafton Streets stood the old inn, occupied as a headquarters by Union general Lew Wallace and, later, by Stonewall Jackson.

On June 11, 1861, Wallace attacked Romney, driving out the Confederates who recaptured the town a few hours later. The town changed hands fifty-six times during the War.

Shepherdstown

Sheets House. At the northwest corner of German and King Streets, William Sheets made gun stocks for use in the Federal Armory at Harpers Ferry. After the Armory was destroyed during the War, Sheets built a picket fence out of his left-over supply of stocks.

Elmwood Cemetery. In the burial ground stands a memorial to 577 Confederate men killed at Antietam, seven miles away in Maryland.

St. Albans

Battle of Scary Creek. A marker recalls the July 17, 1861, encounter, at which Confederates won a victory, although they were soon driven away from the area.

Smoke Hole Caverns

Located on highway 28, eight miles southwest of Petersburg, the caverns were used during the War for storing ammunition.

Summersville

Carnifex Ferry Battlefield State Park. On September 10, 1861, Union general William S. Rosecrans defeated a Confederate unit led by General John B. Floyd. After several hours of fighting, Rosecrans withdrew to await daybreak. Floyd surmised the Union troops intended to cut off his line of retreat, so he proceeded to abandon his positions. The Patterson House Museum at the park, ten miles southwest of Summersville, displays War items.

Nancy Hart. A marker on the courthouse lawn recalls the ravishing twenty-year-old beauty who led a Confederate raid on Summersville in July 1861, capturing the Union unit there. Hart was later captured and put into the local jail where she charmed a guard into letting her examine his pistol. She shot him dead, then escaped to Confederate territory.

Wheeling

West Virginia Independence Hall. Exhibits and a film trace the state's cultural history. Representatives from western Virginia met at the Hall in 1861 to condemn the state's secession. The first Wheeling Convention met to discuss a "New Virginia Now or Never" plan. A second Convention nullified on June 11 the Virginia ordinance of secession and laid plans for a new state, a move overwhelmingly approved in an October 24, 1861, election. By February 18, 1862, the third Wheeling Convention had completed a new constitution. On April 20, 1863, Lincoln issued a proclamation declaring that sixty days later West Virginia would become the thirty-fifth state.

White Sulphur Springs

Battle of White Sulphur Springs. A few miles from the famous spa resort 2000 Confederates clashed with 1300 Union soldiers on August 26-7, 1863. With one-sixth of his men killed or wounded, the Federal commander was forced to retreat.

"Old White." The White Sulphur Springs Hotel, built in 1854 and torn down in 1913, served as headquarters for both sides and as a hospital, with the wounded put in the dining room and the elegant ballroom. Behind the main building stood the Lee Cottage, where Lee and his family spent the summers of 1867, 1868 and 1869.

Willow Hall

McNeill Raiders. Willow Hall, an 1818 mansion in the country near Moorefield, served as the base for Captain Hanson McNeill and his son Jesse, who organized a band of some 200 men to harass Union units. After Confederates lost control of the Baltimore and Ohio line, the pesky raiders destroyed tracks and bridges and captured supply trains. When Hanson was killed by one of his own men in a dispute in October 1864, Jesse took command. In February 1865 he captured two Union generals at Cumberland, Maryland (see that entry).

Other Books by Tom Weil published by Hippocrene...

U.S.A. GUIDE TO AMERICA'S SOUTH
The Atlantic States

"No other guide available covers this area as thoroughly"—Booklist

The guide covers the five coastal southern states, Florida, Georgia, South Carolina, North Carolina and Virginia, and includes a section on the important Civil War sites in those states. With maps and photos this volume introduces readers to the history and culture that makes the South unique.
0-7818-0139-7 $14.95

U.S.A. GUIDE TO AMERICA'S SOUTH
The Gulf and Mississippi States

The spirit and traditions of the Deep South states, Mississippi, Alabama and Louisiana are captured, as well as the border states of Kentucky and Tennessee. A special section explores President Clinton's Arkansas. This book provides outsiders with a glimpse of authentic Southern culture.
0-7818-0171-0 $14.95

THE MISSISSIPPI RIVER
Nature, Culture and Travel Sites along the "Mighty Mississipp"

Following the river's course from its humble beginnings in Minnesota to its mouth in the Gulf of Mexico, Weil offers information on the history and culture of each region and provides itineraries for travelers, who want to explore the towns and cities that developed along the river's banks.
0-7818-0142-7 $16.95

AMERICA'S HEARTLAND
A Travel Guide to the Backroads of Illinois, Indiana, Iowa, Kansas and Missouri

From rustic wineries, old-time villages and century-old covered bridges to modern architecture and bustling cities, Weil has captured the flavor and texture of the heartland through anecdotes and tales of colorful characters. Detailing many little-known sites, this book will delight midwestern natives and those just passing through.
0-7818-0044-7 $14.95

Recently published by Hippocrene...

SPIES AND SPYMASTERS OF THE CIVIL WAR
by Donald E. Markle

The most comprehensive work on the subject ever written,
SPIES AND SPYMASTERS OF THE CIVIL WAR unmasks
the entire history of Civil War espionage, covering the lives,
techniques, successes and failures of all the top Union and
Confederate spies and spymasters.

With an appendix of all known Civil War spies—432 in
all—as well as a glossary of Civil War spy terms, SPIES AND
SPYMASTERS is the ultimate guide to understanding Civil
War espisonage and the foundation it built for modern-day
military intelligence.

Author Donald Markle is an alumnus of the Civil War
Institute at Gettysburg College. A veteran of 34 years in the
U.S. Department of Defense Intelligence, Markle has given
numerous lectures on Civil War espionage.

0-7818-0227-X $24.95

HISTORY & POLITICS
FROM HIPPOCRENE BOOKS

TERRIBLE INNOCENCE:
GENERAL SHERMAN AT WAR
Mark Coburn

In a war of set piece battles, with rivers of blood, General
William Tecumseh Sherman was a striking exception. He
believed that "the time has come when we should attempt
the boldest moves, and my experience is that they are
easier of execution than more timid ones." A master of
logistics, he was most sparing of his men's lives: "night
and day I labor to the end that not a life shall be lost in
vain."

He burnt cities, but he saved lives; the terror he inspired made his victories less expensive in lives and more
effective. Contrary to rumors, Sherman permitted arson
and pillage, but not wanton killing and rape. His army
lived off the land, to make continuing offensives less de-
pendent on uncertain supplies.

A great strategist with an uncanny memory and a feeling for terrain, General Sherman was a fine writer as well.
His orders were dear and to the point, and his memoirs
most readable and accurate. Mark Coburn's account is as
lively and vital as his subject, and does justice to a general
who in his focus on winning and in his thinking was as
modern as General Patton 80 years later.

An escaped New Yorker, Coburn lives in Durango,
Colorado, and teaches English at Fort Lewis College. He
has written many articles on the American past.

MILITARY BOOK CLUB MAIN SELECTION

240 pages, 6 x 9, 16 illustrations, 6 maps
0-7818-0156-7   *$22.50 cloth*

HIPPOCRENE MILITARY LIBRARY

DARK AND CRUEL WAR
Don Lowry

"In the name of common sense, I ask you not to appeal to a just God in such a sacrilegious manner. You who, in the midst of peace and prosperity, have plunged a nation into war-dark and cruel war..." —Major General William Tecumseh Sherman, USA, to General John Bell Hood, CSA

By the fall of the city of Atlanta to Union troops on September 1, 1864, it appeared as if the Civil War would soon end with a Union victory. And yet, the end was still a long way off. In the long and agonizing months before the moment when arms were finally silenced, terrible depredations the likes never seen before or again in American history were to be wrought, a myriad of bloody battles were still to be fought and thousands who yearned for the end had yet to be killed or maimed.

   Dark and Cruel War is a chronicle of this devastating period of the Civil War. As in his previous two volumes, *No Turning Back* and *Fate of the Country*, author Don Lowry ties together the epic campaigns in the eastern and western theaters of the Civil War in this third volume of the series. His narrative captures the climax of the Civil War, and spans from Sherman's mission to "make Georgia howl" to Philip Sheridan's stunning victories in the Shenandoah Valley.

555 pages, 6 x 9
0-7818-0168-0   *$27.50*

HIPPOCRENE MILITARY LIBRARY

FATE OF THE COUNTRY
The Civl War from June to September 1864
Don Lowry

"An excellent account of the period ...
recommended—Booklist
"[Lowry's] frame-by-frame chronology succeeds in
heightening the natural drama of the events."
—Library Journal

555 pages, 6 x 9, index, 4 maps
0-7818-0064-1 $27.50

NO TURNING BACK
The End of the Civil War
May-June 1864
Don Lowry

The first in Lowry's series on the entire Northern campaign
of Ulysses Grant. This day-by-day account explores the
stategies and tactics employed by Grant as Lincoln's general
in chief in the Spring of 1864. Emphasis is placed on the
battles of Wilderness and Spotsylvania.

576 pages, 6 x 9
0-87052-010-5 $27.50

TO PURCHASE HIPPOCRENE'S BOOKS contact your
local bookstore, or write to Hippocrene Books, 171 Madison
Avenue, New York, NY 10016. Please enclose a check or
money order, adding $4.00 shipping (UPS) for the first book,
and $.50 for each additional book.

HIPPOCRENE GUIDE
to

THE UNDERGROUND RAILROAD

Charles L. Blockson

A travel guide and historic reference to over 150 houses, institutions, buildings, and landmarks in the United States and Canada relating to the "Flight to Freedom" experienced by escaping slaves during the antebellum period.

As the chairperson of the advisory committee of the National Park Service, author **Charles Blockson** has been a key participant in the formation of a National Trail of historical markers identifying sites which have been soundly verified for historical accuracy. A native of Norristown, Pennsylvania, Mr. Blockson is curator of the Afro-American Collection that bears his name located at Temple University. The Blockson Collection now contains approximately 80,000 items ranging from books, sheet music and posters to actual shackles and other antebellum artifacts.

82 Black and White Photos, 5 Maps, Glossary, Index
Appendices: Songs of the Underground Railroad, Words and Music
Following the Harriet Tubman Trail: A Suggested Route Tour Specializing in the Sites of the Underground Railroad

$22.95 cloth ISBN 0-7818-0253-9

HIPPOCRENE U.S.A. GUIDES

BLACK NEW YORK
Joann Biondi and James Haskins

New York City carries the highest concentrated population of
African-Americans in the United States. Therefore it follows
that New York should be rich in Black heritage. *Black New
York* takes you by the hand into the heart of the city's Black
communities and explains the significant contributions that
African-Americans have made. Newspapers, jazz joints,
festivals, radio shows, and historic sites are just a few of the
contributions to American society New Yorkers have made.
Harlem, Manhattan, Brooklyn, the Bronx and Queens are
included.

250 pages ISBN 0-7818-0172-9 $14.95

BLACK AMERICA
Marcella Thum

"A useful acquisition for all travel collections."—*Library
Journal*
"An admirable guide."—*Choice Magazine*

Organized by state, this fully indexed guide describes more
that 700 historic homes, art and history museums, parks,
monuments, landmarks of the civil rights movement,
battlefields, colleges and churches across the U.S., all open to
the public.

325 pages ISBN 0-87052-045-8 $11.95

HISTORIC BLACK SOUTH
Joann Biondi and James Haskins

"The book provides some wonderful reading and inspires tourists to go and explore a part of the south that has not been emphasized in travel."
—*Library Journal*

This unique guide describes over 1,000 sites which pay tribute to the significant and often overlooked contribution of the southern African-American community. Read about, then visit, churches, art galleries and jazz clubs, beaches and barbershops, as this guide opens doors to a new appreciation of the historic Black South for all. Includes a description of attractions open to the public, listing hours, fees, directions, and phone numbers.

300 PAGES ISBN 0-7818-0140-0 $14.95

BLACK WASHINGTON
Sandra Fitzpatrick and Maria Goodwin

"The authors provide a much-needed corrective and show how black Washingtonians affected not only this city but the nation and indeed, the world."—*The Washington Post Book World*

Explore over 200 sites in our nation's capital, central to the African-American experience. Gain insight into the heritage that had a profound impact on African-American culture and American society at large, including information about such pivotal figures as Frederick Douglass, Ralph Bunche, Anna J. Cooper, Duke Ellington, and Senator Edward Brooke. From Capitol Hill to Shaw to Lafayette Square to Georgetown, the authors systematically cover the entire city.

288 PAGES ISBN 0-87052-832-7 $14.95

U.S.A. TRAVEL from HIPPOCRENE BOOKS...

AMERICA, A WHERE TO GO GUIDE, by Ken Westcott-Jones
$14.95 • 144 pages • b/w photos, maps • 0-87052-88-2

THE HAWAIIAN ISLANDS, by Carole Chester
$8.95 • 164 pages • b/w photos • 0-87052-341-4

LONG STAYS IN AMERICA, by Roger Hicks and Fran Schultz
$27.50 • 200 pages, hardcover • b/w photos • 0-87052-342-2

PRESIDENTIAL LANDMARKS, by David and Louis Kruh
$24.95 • 480 pages, hardcover • b/w photos • 0-7818-0143-5

UNCOMMON AND UNHERALDED MUSEUMS, by Narkiewicz
& Bates
$14.95 • 131 pages • b\w photos • 0-87052-956-0

NORTHEASTERN TRAVEL

EXPLORING THE BERKSHIRES, *Revised*, by Herbert Whitman,
illustrated by Rosemary Fox
$9.95 • 168 pages • illustrations • 0-87052-979-X

EXPLORING NANTUCKET, by Herbert Whitman, illustrated by
Rosemary Fox
$11.95 • 144 pages • illustrations • 0-87052-792-4

EXPLORING THE LITCHFIELD HILLS, by Herbert Whitman,
illustrated by Rosemary Fox
$11.95 • 165 pages • illustrations • 0-7818-0045-5

**LONG ISLAND: A Guide to New York's Suffolk and Nassau
Counties,** *Revised*, by Raymond Spinzia
$17.50 • 250 pages • maps • 0-87052-879-3

WESTPOINT AND THE HUDSON VALLEY, by Gale Kohlhagen
and Ellen Heinbach
$14.95 • 320 pages • b/w photos, illust. • 0-87052-889-0

MIDWESTERN TRAVEL

EXPLORING MID-AMERICA: A Guide to Museum Villages, by Gerald and Patricia Gutek
$14.95 • 172 pages • b/w photos • 0-87052-643-X

CHICAGOLAND & BEYOND, by Gerald and Patricia Gutek
$14.95 • 288 pages • maps, b/w photos • 0-87052-036-9

SOUTHERN TRAVEL

THE KEY TO FLORIDA: A City Breaks Guide, by Reg Butler
$7.95 • 112 pages • maps •0-87052-178-0

WESTERN TRAVEL

THE ROCKY MOUNTAIN STATES, by Henry Weisser
$14.95 • 366 pages • b/wphotos • 0-7818-0043-9

THE SOUTHWEST: A Family Adventure, by Tish Minear and Janet Limon
$16.95 • 440 pages • b/w photos, illust. • 0-87052-640-5

(Prices subject to change.)

TO PURCHASE HIPPOCRENE BOOKS, contact your local bookstore, or write to: HIPPOCRENE BOOKS, 171 madison Avenue, New York, NY 10016. Please enclose check or money order, adding $4.00 shipping (UPS) for the first book and .50 for each additional book.